KU-532-709

New Casebooks

VILLETTE

New Casebooks

PUBLISHED
Hamlet
Middlemarch
Tristram Shandy
Macbeth
Villette

FORTHCOMING
Emma
Sense and Sensibility and *Pride and Prejudice*
Jane Eyre
Wuthering Heights
Great Expectations
Tess of the D'Urbervilles
Jude The Obscure
To the Lighthouse and *Mrs Dalloway*
Sons and Lovers
Ulysses
Waiting for Godot and *Endgame*
Chaucer
Metaphysical Poetry
Wordsworth
Blake
Shakespeare's History Plays
King Lear
Antony and Cleopatra

New Casebooks

VILLETTE

CHARLOTTE BRONTË

EDITED BY PAULINE NESTOR

© Pauline Nestor 1992

Published by
PALGRAVE MACMILLAN
Houndmills, Basingstoke, Hampshire RG21 6XS and
175 Fifth Avenue, New York, N. Y. 10010
Companies and representatives throughout the world

PALGRAVE MACMILLAN is the global academic imprint of the Palgrave Macmillan division of St. Martin's Press, LLC and of Palgrave Macmillan Ltd. Macmillan® is a registered trademark in the United States, United Kingdom and other countries. Palgrave is a registered trademark in the European Union and other countries.

ISBN-13: 978– 0–333–55137–0 hardback
ISBN-10: 0–333–55137–0   hardback
ISBN-13: 978–0–333–55138–7 paperback
ISBN-10: 0–333–55138–9   paperback

This book is printed on paper suitable for recycling and made from fully managed and sustained forest sources.

A catalogue record for this book is available from the British Library.

Printed and bound in Great Britain by
Antony Rowe Ltd, Chippenham and Eastbourne

Contents

v

Acknowledgements

The editor and publishers wish to thank the following for permission to use copyright material:

Terry Eagleton, extract from *Myths of Power* (1975). Copyright © 1975 by Terry Eagleton, by permission of Macmillan, London and Basingstoke and HarperCollins Publishers Inc.;

Sandra Gilbert and Susan Gubar, extracts from *The Madwoman in the Attic: The Woman Writer and the Nineteenth-Century Literary Imagination* (1979), by permission of Yale University Press;

Mary Jacobus, extracts from *Reading Woman: Essays in Feminist Criticism*, Methuen & Co. (1986), by permission of Routledge;

Kate Millett, extract from *Sexual Politics*, Granada (1971), by permission of Georges Borchardt, Inc. on behalf of the author;

Helene Moglen, extract from *Charlotte Brontë: The Self Conceived* (1976), by permission of the University of Wisconsin;

Nancy Sorkin Rabinowitz, '"Faithful Narrator" or "Partial Eulogist": First-Person Narration in Brontë's *Villette*', *Journal of Narrative Technique*, 15 (Fall 1985), by permission of the Journal of Narrative Technique;

Sally Shuttleworth, '"The Surveillance of a Sleepless Eye": The Constitution of Neurosis in *Villette*' in *One Culture: Essays in Science and Literature*, ed. George Levine (1987), by permission of the University of Wisconsin Press;

Brenda Silver, 'The Reflecting Reader in *Villette*' in *The Voyage in: Fictions of Female Development*, eds Elizabeth Abel *et al.* (1983). Copyright © 1983 by Trustees of Dartmouth College, by permission of University Press of New England;

Tony Tanner, extracts from 'Introduction' to *Villette* by Charlotte Brontë, Penguin Classics (1979). Copyright © 1979 Tony Tanner, by permission of Penguin Books Ltd.

Every effort has been made to trace all the copyright holders but if any have been inadvertently overlooked the publishers will be pleased to make the necessary arrangement at the first opportunity.

General Editors' Preface

The purpose of this new series of Casebooks is to reveal some of the ways in which contemporary criticism has changed our understanding of commonly studied texts and writers and, indeed, of the nature of criticism itself. Central to the series is a concern with modern critical theory and its effect on current approaches to the study of literature. Each New Casebook editor has been asked to select a sequence of essays which will introduce the reader to the new critical approaches to the text or texts being discussed in the volume and also illuminate the rich interchange between critical theory and critical practice that characterises so much current writing about literature.

The series itself, of course, grows out of the original Casebook series edited by A. E. Dyson. The original volumes provide readers with a range of critical opinions extending from the first reception of a work through to the criticism of the twentieth century. By contrast, the focus of the New Casebooks is on modern critical thinking and practice, with the volumes seeking to reflect both the controversy and the excitement of current criticism. Because much of this criticism is difficult and often employs an unfamiliar critical language, editors have been asked to give the reader as much help as they feel is appropriate, but without simplifying the essays or the issues they raise.

The project of the New Casebooks, then, is to bring together in an illuminating way those critics who best illustrate the ways in which contemporary criticism has established new methods of analysing texts and who have reinvigorated the important debate about how we 'read' literature. The hope is, of course, that New Casebooks will not only open up this debate to a wider audience, but will also encourage students to extend their own ideas, and think afresh about their responses to the texts they are studying.

John Peck and Martin Coyle
University of Wales, Cardiff

Introduction

PAULINE NESTOR

I

While Charlotte Brontë enjoyed remarkable success during her lifetime, her reputation was gradually eclipsed in the century after her death by her sister Emily's, so that by 1960 there was critical consensus on the comparatively minor significance of Charlotte's novels measured against the greatness of *Wuthering Heights*.[1] Since then, however, there has been something of a resurgence in Charlotte's critical reputation and this has coincided with an explosion of interest in the last 20 years in new critical theories which have substantially altered the way in which we read literary texts. Poststructuralism, for example, has problematised any assumptions of a direct and simple relationship between author, text and reader, and deconstruction, one variant of poststructuralism which draws on the insights of psychoanalysis, has disrupted any sense of the possibility of fixed meaning and called into question the seeming integrity of the realist text and the unity of its subject. Similarly, discourse theory has challenged any claim to an objective knowledge of history, and Marxism and feminism have drawn attention to the inescapably political nature of writing and reading.

As new critical theories have developed it has become clear that different texts lend themselves more and less readily to different theoretical approaches. The apparently seamless prose of the realist text, for example, provides less fertile ground for poststructuralist readings of the gaps, silences and disruptions of the 'text's unconscious' than the modernist text which foregrounds its fictiveness and draws attention to its existence as a literary construct. However, it would be a mistake to imagine that the realist novel cannot be illuminated by poststructuralism, for as the tenets of deconstruction would have it, *all* utterance has within it the potential for its own subversion, and in any case, as Mary Jacobus's deconstructive reading of *Villette* in this volume argues, even the realism of Brontë's text cannot simply be taken for granted, since its narrative and representational conventions 'are constantly threatened by an incompletely repressed Romanticism'.[2]

Perhaps the single most influential factor in the re-estimation of Brontë's work has been the emergence of feminist literary theory. To acknowledge this, however, is not to isolate a single approach to Brontë's fiction, for feminist literary theory is as eclectic in its critical practice as it is diverse in its range of political positions. Just as feminism ranges across an ideological spectrum from liberalism to radicalism, so its literary theory draws on a variety of theoretical positions from New Criticism to deconstruction and New Historicism. Thus, at the one extreme it encompasses quite traditional aesthetic values such as a belief in the authority of the author and in the ethical and intellectual relevance of the text to life, and a concern for textual harmony and wholeness, while at the other extreme it involves a denial both of the fixity of meaning and of the author as the originator of meaning and a concern to highlight the contradictions and inconsistencies of the text.

II

The first extract in this volume comes from Helene Moglen's critical biography, *Charlotte Brontë: The Self Conceived*. Moglen's study is modern both in its conviction that Brontë's growth was indicative of 'the nature of the feminist struggle' and in its application of psychoanalytic principles to its analysis. In its concern for Brontë's life and the way in which that life is 'transmuted into fiction', though, Moglen's work takes its place in a long tradition of biographically based studies which stretch all the way back to Elizabeth Gaskell's *Life of Charlotte Brontë* which appeared two years after Brontë's death in 1857.[3] Yet, whereas influential critics such as Leslie Stephen in the 1880s and Lord David Cecil in the 1930s have used a simple conflation of the life and the literature to denigrate Brontë's work as involuntary self-revelation rather than deliberate self-diagnosis,[4] Moglen argues that Brontë transcends the limitations of the merely personal in her fiction, dramatising the conflict of 'larger social and psychological forces' and offering 'visionary' insight into psychosexual relationships.[5]

In keeping with the psychological focus of her work, Moglen's piece is primarily concerned with character study and the 'psychological validity of Brontë's insight'.[6] Moglen sees Lucy Snowe's development as an exemplary struggle toward emotional maturity in which her psychic health is dependent upon her negotiation of the perils on the one hand of sexual expression and on the other of sexual repression, represented *in extremis* in the novel by the figures of Vashti and the nun respectively. Throughout the discussion Moglen characterises the creative act of Brontë's fiction as essentially therapeutic. So, she argues that Paul Emanuel, though offering some 'promise of equality',[7] is the type of the Byronic hero who haunted Brontë's life and fiction, and that his failure to return to Lucy at the end of the novel is crucial to the development of both heroine and author:

> He could not return because Brontë's fantasy relationship with Heger would not then have been laid to rest. The Belgian's idealisation would not have been balanced by his irrecoverable loss. The tragic circumstances of her life would have been denied. No matter how great her desire and how firm her wish to believe, no matter how unprepared she was to confront directly the irreducible fact of Heger's indifference, Brontë could not betray the larger reality of her experience.[8]

The second extract in this volume is from Kate Millett's *Sexual Politics*, a pioneering work of feminist criticism which appeared in 1970 and which, through an examination of nineteenth- and twentieth-century history and literature, explored the workings of 'sexual politics' – the process, according to Millett, by which males seek to maintain sexual dominion over females.[9] Millett's discussion is provocatively polemical, energised by a consciously disrespectful and confrontational style. Contrary to the tenets of New Criticism which prevailed in the 1960s, Millett insisted that literature had to be understood in relation to its social and cultural context. This endeavour to recontextualise literature formed an important strategy for early feminist criticism since, as Virginia Woolf had brilliantly contemplated in *A Room of One's Own*, the social and material conditions under which women wrote, or failed to write, have had a decisive effect on the nature of our literary inheritance.

In contrast to some of the more recent critics in this volume Millett assumes that literature has a straightforward and unproblematic relevance to life. Thus, she sees the novel's female characters as monitory types of patriarchal distortion. Lucy, for example, is a 'neurotic revolutionary' whose character illustrates the effects that life 'in a male-supremacist society has upon the psyche of a woman'. Nonetheless, in a move characteristic of early feminist criticism, Millett values the heroine for her inspirational power. Lucy is seen to represent not only Brontë's desire for freedom, knowledge and a sense of purpose but that 'of every conscious young woman in the world'.[10] Mrs Bretton, in contrast, 'stands for a stale and selfless maternity', Madame Beck is the 'tireless functionary of European sexual inhibition' and Paulina Home represents the infantilised 'perfect woman' of patriarchal society. The males, similarly, are seen as recognisable types. Graham Bretton is 'the delightful and infuriating egotist whom maturity means learning to relinquish one's "crush" on', while Paul Emanuel represents 'the male one encounters a bit later in life when one tries to make one's way ... the voice of piety, conventionality, male supremacy, callow chauvinism terrified of female competition'.[11]

Like all the critics in this volume, Millett is struck by the division and contradictoriness in *Villette*. She interprets it, however, in a way that assumes that the author is in full control of her text. Indeed, Millett isolates the novel's 'astonishing degree of consciousness' as its most satisfying feature. In these terms contradictoriness is read as illustrative rather than symptomatic, and division is read as a technique consciously employed by Brontë both to reflect and expose the 'social schizophrenia within masculine culture'.[12] Similarly, Millett regards the ambiguous or 'open' ending of the novel as an enabling 'solution' which allows Brontë to appease the dictates of Victorian convention while granting her heroine the prospect of escape from the prison of patriarchal strictures.

The third extract in this volume comes from Sandra Gilbert and Susan Gubar's *The Madwoman in the Attic*, a highly influential text in American feminist criticism of the late 1970s. Gilbert and Gubar's vast study of the nineteenth-century female literary imagination advances the thesis that female authors have been compelled to work within a patriarchal ideology which represents the creative act as masculine and hence condemns women who venture the pen to a potentially debilitating 'anxiety of authorship'.[13] As a consequence, women have produced strategically duplicitous works, as though heeding the advice of Emily Dickinson to 'Tell all the Truth but tell it slant'. Gilbert and Gubar read nineteenth-century women's texts, then, as 'palimpsestic', presenting a surface which disguises 'less accessible (and less socially acceptable) levels of meaning', and thus managing 'the difficult task of achieving true female literary authority by simultaneously conforming to and subverting patriarchal literary standards'.[14]

Like a number of early feminist accounts, Gilbert and Gubar's reading sees Lucy's narrative as the struggle to find a voice through which the heroine develops away from evasion toward self-articulation and self-dramatisation. However, in keeping with their general thesis about the restrictive nature of the patriarchal forms available to women, they argue that Lucy's is not simply a psychological struggle but an aesthetic one. In this the parallel between Lucy's role as narrator and Brontë's as creator is clear – for both, self-representation, and hence identity, is dependent upon the attempt to create 'an adequate fiction'.[15]

Gilbert and Gubar argue that the novel's critique of patriarchal aesthetic forms takes place at the level both of form and content. In formal terms the heroine's dilemma is seen as arising from the fact that her life and her sense of self do not conform to the 'literary or social stereotypes provided by her culture to define and circumscribe female life'.[16] Hence the evasive and duplicitous style of Lucy's narrative can be read both as a reaction to those limitations and an indictment of them. In its content the novel provides a further critique of the culture's confining aesthetic conventions through the presentation of Lucy's visit to the art gallery, where she views the portrait of the voluptuous Cleopatra and the didactic sequence of '*La vie d'une femme*', and to the civic concert, where the pomp and circumstance blind all but Lucy to the human drama surrounding the King's illness. In both episodes the arts are revealed as 'egotistical and coercive', co-opted in the service of perpetuating 'the false myths that insure the continuance of patriarchal forms'.[17]

The inflammatory performance of Vashti also searingly exposes the hypocrisy of such forms. However, in its excess – a form of 'female suicidal self-exposure'[18] – the figure of Vashti reveals the dangers of the unbridled imagination. Gilbert and Gubar conclude that with the monitory image of the rebel Vashti before her, Lucy must recognise both the need for imaginative self-projection and its limitations.

Ironically, Gilbert and Gubar's book has been criticised for its reliance on 'patriarchal aesthetics'. Both Mary Jacobus and Toril Moi, for example, argue that Gilbert and Gubar construct the woman writer as the authoritative source, or 'transcendental signified', of the text and thus implicate themselves in patriarchal concern with the assertions of fixed identity and authority.[19] The conservative implications of such a position have been highlighted by the structuralist Roland Barthes in his influential essay, 'The Death of the Author':

> To give a text an Author is to impose a limit on that text, to furnish it with a final signified, to close the writing. Such a conception suits criticism very well, the latter then allotting itself the important task of discovering the Author (or its hypostases: society, history, psyche, liberty) beneath the work: when the Author has been found, the text is 'explained' – victory to the critic.

It is only when the Author is removed, Barthes contends, that the 'claim to decipher a text becomes quite futile', the impulse to assign an 'ultimate meaning' to a text is abandoned, and criticism becomes 'truly revolutionary'.[20]

Moi also objects to Gilbert and Gubar's representation of the woman writer as an 'integrated humanist individual' rather than the divided or fragmented subject who challenges phallogocentric conceptions of identity. Furthermore, in criticism that might equally apply to Kate Millett, Moi points out that Gilbert and Gubar see patriarchal ideology as monolithic and non-contradictory and yet fail to account for the curious immunity which allows women to write subversively.[21]

Even allowing for the force of such criticism, Gilbert and Gubar's work in *The Madwoman in the Attic* nonetheless represented a significant advance in the theoretical sophistication of feminist criticism, moving beyond a concern with character, theme and plot alone, to attempt to theorise women's literary creativity and to provide an account of feminist poetics.

III

The next three essays in this volume by Tony Tanner, Nancy Sorkin Rabinowitz and Brenda Silver are particularly concerned with the narrative act itself, and although they each have distinctly different emphases, they all offer close formalist readings and draw to an extent on theories of narratology devised by Russian formalist and structuralist critics.

Tony Tanner's starting point in 'Reading Reality in *Villette*' is perhaps the most traditional. He views Brontë's novel as 'a study in how a human being attempts to constitute herself in a society largely indifferent to her needs' and considers the literary critical act as a humanising one, a way of enabling readers 'to return to our own condition with a heightened awareness'.[22] Given Tanner's sympathetic reading of the novel, questions of the particular relevance of gender inevitably do arise and in the longer piece from which this extract comes Tanner does consider the 'exceptionally difficult' position of the woman novelist in the nineteenth century and the problems of self-definition for women who are 'constantly being defined by men' and required to work with a language which is 'already full of male imperatives, classifications, pre-definitions, and arbitrary cultural oppositions'.[23] However, Tanner's emphasis is predominantly humanist rather than feminist and the novel remains for him an exploration of the 'human drama', a drama based 'very much on lack and need'.[24] Tanner sees *Villette* as a precursor to modern philosophical preoccupations with the 'lack' or 'ontological privation' which both characterises human existence and provides the origin of action.

Tanner's concern with the notion of lack needs to be distinguished, however, from that of deconstructionist critics. In his discussion Tanner invokes the theories of the French existentialist and humanist philosopher Jean-Paul Sartre who, while diagnosing the individual's inclination to live in 'bad faith', nonetheless held out the prospect of living in 'good faith', of arriving at 'some definitive state of being'.[25] At least ideally, then, in this state of 'authentic' being, the 'lack' or 'need' might be satisfied. Such a view is diametrically opposed to that of another French theorist, the psychoanalyst Jacques Lacan, whose work has been extensively drawn on by deconstructionist critics. From an essentially anti-humanist position Lacan maintains that identity is formed through lack – that the individual's capacity to assume a subject position, to say 'I am', is dependent upon her capacity to recognise 'I am that which I am not' – and that the notion of an 'authentic' unified self is entirely mythic.

Tanner's focus on the notion of 'being' translates into a preoccupation with the narrative act because, in the terms of his argument, Lucy 'can only be herself to the extent that she can speak herself'.[26] Lucy's drama, then, is acted out at the level of language. Her constriction within 'bourgeois boundaries' is represented through spatial, particularly architectural, metaphors, and her liberation comes through the exploration of aberrational states of dream, hallucination and apparition. So, for example, Lucy's drugged night walk through the scenes of the festival is described by Tanner as a 'venture beyond the conventional cognitive frame'.[27] In this shifting, duplicitous world of 'substance and shadow' in *Villette* there are no epistemological certainties for Lucy. Her narrative thus becomes more than the record of her life, for by her interpretative act Lucy creates her own ontology and value system, and through the exploration of states of mind 'on the extreme edge of mental disorder', Tanner suggests that Charlotte Brontë is able to offer 'new "readings" of reality, which slip away from the constraining bourgeois house of consciousness . . . just as Lucy slips away from Mme Beck's house in the night'.[28]

In her essay '"Faithful Narrator" or "Partial Eulogist": First-Person Narration in Brontë's *Villette*' Nancy Rabinowitz shares Tony Tanner's reading of the narrative as a reaction against confinement, but whereas Tanner tends to see such confinement as 'bourgeois' constriction, Rabinowitz sees it in more insistently feminist terms as the attempt to 'alter male forms' and hence to 'avoid male constructions of female experience'.[29] Drawing on Nancy Miller's feminist critique of the 'blind spot' in criticism which takes masculine 'fictions of desire' to represent a 'universal' reality,[30] Rabinowitz reads Lucy's notoriously unreliable narrative as an attempt to escape the conventional dictates of the realistic form. Rabinowitz considers the examples of Lucy's deceptions in detail and concludes that they form the basis of a 'strategy of denial'[31] which provides Lucy with a means to power. Lucy prefers to remain silent and leave herself unexplained on occasion because in a world where she lacks the power to make herself known and understood, she can at least assume the negative power of refusing to collaborate with this misunderstanding by withholding information. In this way, too, she can retain some measure of privacy in an environment which is characterised by invasive surveillance and spying. Similarly, Lucy's deceptions toward the reader can be read as the demonstration of the only real power Lucy has available to her – the power over her own narrative. It is particularly in this 'misuse' of language that Lucy foregrounds her capacity for control, since, as Rabinowitz points out, whereas language may be used conventionally to give the appearance of straightforward referentiality or transparency, we are in fact made much more aware of the power of language 'when it deceives us or leads us astray'.[32]

The next essay, Brenda Silver's 'The Reflecting Reader in *Villette*', takes issue with the common critical observations about Lucy

INTRODUCTION 9

Snowe's unreliability as a narrator, suggesting instead that Lucy is 'self-consciously reliable', and that it is really the question of 'plausibility' that needs to be examined. Drawing, like Rabinowitz, on Nancy Miller's work on women's narrative, Silver argues that women's texts have been misread as extravagant or implausible because they are judged by the inappropriate criteria of the dominant cultural ideology. So, for example, the apparent silences of a text may be an indication of the inadequacy of the 'dominant mode of reception', for which the text's 'alternative ideology' may 'simply be inaudible'.[33]

Like Tanner and Rabinowitz, Silver sees Lucy's identity as constituted by her role as narrator and recognises the need for Lucy to create a 'new reality'. However, she maintains that this struggle to create a new form of fiction is inextricably linked to the necessity of creating a new audience. In keeping with Wolfgang Iser's theories of 'reader response', Silver argues that narrative exists as the 'mutual creation of the text and its readers',[34] an act of negotiation that depends upon the author's ability to stimulate the reader's imagination to new ways of seeing. Silver traces the existence of an 'implied reader' in the text and argues that Lucy actually begins her tale with two readers – the first, a potentially antagonistic conventional or socialised reader, and the second, a more sympathetic rebellious or unsocialised reader. This split in the audience is seen as a reflection of Lucy's inner conflict between realism and rebellion – her struggle to 'compromise between her necessarily unconventional actions and her need to remain within the social structure'.[35]

Applying Gérard Genette's structuralist categorisation of narrative form into three types – the 'plausible narrative' which conforms to the conventions of the genre and the cultural maxims on which they rest, the 'arbitrary narrative' which deliberately destroys this collusion but refuses to justify itself, and the narrative of 'motivated' or 'artificial' plausibility which justifies its story by 'providing the missing maxims, or by inventing them' – Silver argues that Lucy's tale might properly be read as a combination of the second and third types, an alternation between a self-consciously created 'artificially plausible' narrative directed at the socialised reader and an 'arbitrary' narrative directed at the rebellious reader with whom Lucy assumes, and therefore does not attempt to justify, a shared unconventional perspective.[36]

Throughout the course of the novel this 'arbitrary' narrative gradually comes to dominate the text, for as Lucy's sense of herself evolves, the two opposed readers become merged into one. Lucy trains or co-opts the reader by mocking fictional and social conventions and thereby challenging the reader to abandon those in favour of Lucy's perceptions. Silver concludes that this creation of an audience, and hence of a context in which Lucy's strength can be read, is an act of self-survival for the heroine since, as Lucy herself recognises, her existence depends on her capacity 'to acknowledge and share her perceptions of reality'.[37]

IV

All the essays so far discussed celebrate the artistry of Charlotte Brontë and thus by implication posit the existence of some degree of authorial control of the text. Behind this lies the fundamental assumption that the subject/author speaks, rather than is spoken by, language. In addition, the first six essays, while all attending to the divided, contradictory nature of the text, offer readings which work toward understanding or reconciling those divisions, so that the text can be read toward a kind of coherence. The last three essays challenge the notion of the author as the transcendent source of meaning and any sense of the organic wholeness of the text. They are, however, quite diverse in their critical orientation with Terry Eagleton presenting a Marxist reading, Mary Jacobus a deconstructionist analysis and Sally Shuttleworth a New Historicist account. All three critics work from the theoretical assumption that the text betrays other meanings in much the same way as the unconscious disrupts and betrays the conscious mind and they read 'symptomatically' in order to highlight those tensions and disruptions.

Terry Eagleton's essay, like much feminist criticism, has an overtly political agenda, endeavouring to give 'some intelligible account of the relation of literature to the social order'. However, as a Marxist, Eagleton takes class rather than gender as his starting point. In his *Myths of Power: A Marxist Study of the Brontës*, the book from which this essay comes, Eagleton seeks to identify a recurring 'categorical structure' of roles, values and relations through which to identify 'the inner ideological structure of a work, and to expose its relations both to what we call literary "form" and an actual history'. Accordingly, he sees Charlotte Brontë's work as marked by a constant struggle between an individualistic, radical impulse toward protest and rebellion and an affirmation of habits of piety, submission and conservatism. Her novels work toward, but never achieve, a mythic balance or fusion of 'blunt bourgeois rationality and flamboyant Romanticism, brash initiative and genteel cultivation, passionate rebellion and cautious conformity', oppositions which Eagleton sees as embodying 'a complex structure of convergence and antagonism between the landed and industrial sectors of the contemporary ruling class'.[38]

Eagleton reads *Villette*, then, as a novel torn between 'pious submission and defiant rebellion'. The resentment that makes Lucy a 'latent rebel' is checked by 'the overriding need to celebrate bourgeois security'.[39] This conflict in Lucy is played out in her ambiguous dealings with other characters in the book. Her judgments of Graham and Paulina, for example, though ostensibly detached and dismissive, are marked by the jealousy of one excluded from the fortunate life of the Bretton household. Similarly, Lucy's feelings for Mme Beck are torn between admiring her as a role model, a woman who works the system so well, and resenting her as an oppressor, one who constantly infringes upon Lucy's personal liberty.

Mary Jacobus in her essay 'The Buried Letter: Feminism and Romanticism in *Villette*' is concerned not simply with the ways in which the novel is about repression but with the manner in which repression is actually manifest at a formal level in the text as 'incoherencies and compromises, inconsistencies and dislocations'. Whereas critics like Gilbert and Gubar, and Nancy Rabinowitz have argued that Brontë's novel strains to extend the conventions of realism, Jacobus alters the emphasis by suggesting that this strain is the result of 'an incompletely repressed Romanticism'. Applying the terms of psychoanalysis, she contends that this disruptive Romanticism forms 'the discourse of the Other' in the work, 'the novel's unconscious'.[40]

Reading the prose for 'symptoms', such as 'the agitated notation and heightened language' that marks the description of Vashti, Jacobus argues that the text is haunted by a 'sub-text' which eloquently inscribes a critique of Victorian sexual ideology which it cannot explicitly speak. This 'dream-text' challenges the authority of the novel's overarching realism. Thus Lucy's 'dream-like propulsion' through the text, which Terry Eagleton reads as a strategy to construct Lucy as an innocent victim and thereby exonerate her from suspicion of aggressive ambition, Jacobus sees quite differently as the suspension of the 'laws of probability for those of the mind'. In this way the narrative dislocation in *Villette* can be read as an insistence on 'the irreducible otherness, the strangeness and arbitrariness of inner experience'.[41] Drawing on Freud's theories of the uncanny, Jacobus reads the uncertainty created by the novel's dream states as constituting a challenge to the 'monopolistic claims of realism on "reality"'. In these terms she sees the figure of the nun, for example, as symbolising fiction's capacity to evade the censorship of realism.

In her analysis Jacobus takes issue with critics like Kate Millett, who propose 'an unmediated relationship between author and work', and argues that though the novel might invite the reader to make a 'covert identification between Charlotte Brontë and her creation', it simultaneously frustrates that identification by the shifting unreliability of Lucy's narrative.[42] Read psychoanalytically, Lucy is guilty of a classic form of evasion – displacement – in her tendency to narrate the stories of others. Jacobus likens Lucy's tendency to define herself through other characters in the novel to the Lacanian 'mirror-phase' – that is, the way in which we construct a sense of identity from the reflection we see in the mirror (or in the images of self 'reflected' back to us from others). In this way our sense of self does not emanate from some core or essential identity but rather is constructed only in relation to the not-self or Other. The absence, then, at the centre of the subject's constructed identity is mirrored in Brontë's novel by the 'absence' of its shadow-like heroine at its centre.

In a move characteristic of deconstructive criticism, Jacobus argues that instead of 'correcting the novel into a false coherence' the reader should recognise its 'ruptured and ambiguous discourse' as the source of its 'uncanny power'. Its ambiguous ending, she contends, confirms the fact that 'there can be no firm ground; only a perpetual de-centring activity'.[43]

The final essay in this volume, Sally Shuttleworth's '"The Surveillance of a Sleepless Eye": The Constitution of Neurosis in *Villette*', provides a New Historicist reading of Brontë's novel. New Historicism shares with poststructuralism a belief in the inherently contradictory nature of language, evident, for example, in Shuttleworth's contention that the text frustrates any quest for 'a hidden unitary meaning'.[44] However, unlike much of the a-contextual analysis of poststructualism, it seeks to read the text in its historical and discursive context. Indeed, like much Marxist and recent feminist criticism, New

Historicism views the text as a 'site of struggle' which in its contradictions is both a product and a reflection of the tensions inherent in the political and social structure from which it emerges.

Shuttleworth's essay is particularly concerned with reading *Villette* in the context of the social and scientific discourses on psychology in the mid-Victorian period. In a detailed discussion of scientific and popular writing on the subject, Shuttleworth considers the way in which the categorising of neurosis and insanity lent the authority of science to sexual stereotypes of the period. She then goes on to consider the extent to which the novel both 'absorbs and resists the definitions and codifications of female experience'[45] offered by the male medical establishment.

Lucy provides the obvious focus for Shuttleworth's discussion both because she is pathologised by others, subjected in turn to the surveillance of the medical, social and religious establishments, and because she can be seen to internalise the mechanisms of control to which she is exposed and to employ the language of contemporary science in her analysis of self. However, as Shuttleworth argues, at the same time as Lucy uses this language, she also subverts it. In an argument which has parallels with Mary Jacobus's analysis, Shuttleworth examines the way in which Lucy's narrative merges the literal and figural, dissolving the 'divisions between inner psychological life and the material social world', and thus offering an alternative vision which 'challenges the normative psychological vision implicit in male definitions of the "Real"'.[46] Like Jacobus, Shuttleworth reads the novel not as the triumphant affirmation of an essential self but as a recognition that identity is a construct rather than a given, the result of 'a tenuous process of negotiation between the subject and the surrounding social forces'.[47]

The diversity of readings in this volume may be taken as an indication both of the richness of Brontë's text and the lively state of Brontë criticism. Some theoretical positions such as Marxism and feminism are potentially complementary, while others such as traditional humanism and deconstruction are contradictory and mutually exclusive. Perhaps most importantly this volume should indicate that critical readings are not simply alert to the politics of the text but are in themselves essentially political. Indeed, the volume will have served its purpose if, in the words of Mary Jacobus, it works to unsettle 'the illusory objectivity of criticism'.[48]

NOTES

1. See, for example, D. W. Crompton, 'The New Criticism: a Caveat', *Essays in Criticism*, 1.10 (1960), 359–64.

2. See p. 121 below.

3. Helene Moglen, *Charlotte Brontë: The Self Conceived* (New York, 1976), p. 14.

4. Leslie Stephen on Charlotte Brontë, *Cornhill Magazine* (Dec. 1877), in Miriam Allott (ed.), *The Brontës: a Critical Heritage* (London, 1974), pp. 413–23; David Cecil, *Early Victorian Novelists: Essays in Revaluation* (1934; reprinted London, 1960), pp. 109–44.

5. Helene Moglen, *Charlotte Brontë: The Self Conceived* (New York, 1976), p. 145.

6. See p. 21 below.

7. See p. 17 below.

8. See p. 27 below.

9. Kate Millett, *Sexual Politics* (New York, 1970), p. 25.

10. See pp. 32, 37 below.

11. See pp. 34, 33 below.

12. See pp. 41, 37 below.

13. Sandra Gilbert and Susan Gubar, *The Madwoman in the Attic: The Woman Writer and the Nineteenth-Century Literary Imagination* (New Haven, 1979), p. 49.

14. Ibid., p. 73.

15. See p. 45 below.

16. See p. 44 below.

17. See p. 47 below.

18. See p. 49 below.

19. Toril Moi, *Sexual/Textual Politics* (London, 1985), pp. 69, 62. See also Mary Jacobus, Review of *The Madwoman in the Attic, Signs*, 6:3 (1981), 517–23.

20. Roland Barthes, *Image Music Text*, trans. Stephen Heath (London, 1984), p. 147.

21. Toril Moi, *Sexual/Textual Politics* (London, 1985), p. 66.

22. See pp. 58, 59 below.

23. Tony Tanner, Introduction to the Penguin edition of *Villette* (London, 1979), p. 45.

INTRODUCTION 15

24. See p. 59 below.
25. See p. 58 below.
26. Tony Tanner, Introduction to Penguin *Villette* (London, 1979), p. 42.
27. See p. 63 below.
28. See p. 61 below.
29. See p. 69 below.
30. See Nancy K. Miller, 'Emphasis Added: Plots and Plausibilities in Women's Fiction', *PMLA* 96:1 (1981), 36–48.
31. See p. 79 below.
32. See p. 73 below.
33. See p. 85 below.
34. See p. 83 below. See also Wolfgang Iser, *The Implied Reader* (Baltimore, 1974).
35. See p. 87 below.
36. See pp. 84, 85 below.
37. See p. 95 below.
38. Terry Eagleton, *Myths of Power: A Marxist Study of the Brontës* (London, 1975), pp. 2, 4.
39. See pp. 112, 116 below.
40. See pp. 138, 121, 122, below.
41. See pp. 126, 122, 126, 127, 127 below.
42. See pp. 122 below.
43. See pp. 134 below.
44. See p. 143 below.
45. See p. 141 below.
46. See pp. 153, 159 below.
47. See p. 159 below.
48. See p. 138 below.

1

'Villette': the Romantic Experience as Psychoanalysis

HELENE MOGLEN

Having explored the frustrations of her current relationship with George Smith [through her depiction in *Villette* of the relationship between Lucy Snowe and Graham Bretton], Brontë went further back – to that more profound and traumatic relationship which had sparked her to growth and to despair. The movement is progressive in psychoanalytic terms, but regressive in its suggestion that the idealised professor in Brussels became again for Brontë the standard by which all other men had to be judged. It is, of course, through her love affair with Paul Emanuel, the schoolmaster modelled upon M. Heger, that Lucy ultimately realises herself. The pattern of their interaction is similar to that of the 'Jane' poem, which had been repeated in Frances's relationship to Crimsworth, in Jane's relation to Rochester, in Shirley's relation to Louis. Now the psychological process that shaped the pattern is more insightfully presented and the emotional power that informed Brontë's love for her 'maitre' finds expression.

M. Paul has undeniable connections with the Byronic hero. He is 'a dark little man ... pungent and austere' (p. 110), fiery and grasping. He has dark hair, a 'broad, sallow brow' and thin cheek, a 'wide and quivering nostril'. He utters groans of scorn and fierce hisses of rage. Lucy, seeing his love of power, compares him to Napoleon. She comprehends his capacity for deep and irrational passion, the volatility of his temper, his jealousy. A rebel at heart, he fervently opposes tyranny and resists whatever is obligatory. But there is another side to his character. He is benevolent and charitable, given to acts of extraordinary kindness. If 'he was as capricious as women are said to be' (p. 279), he is also as emotional, as sympathetic, as impulsive, and intuitive.

> [His heart] was not an ossified organ: in its core was a place, tender beyond man's tenderness; a place that humbled him to little children, that bound him to girls and women: to whom, rebel as he would, he could not disown his affinity, nor quite deny that, on the whole, he was better with them than with his own sex.
>
> (p. 287)

His is an androgynous nature: not confused and blocked as Hunsworth's was, not insecure as Crimsworth's; but complex and whole. He is the romantic hero humanised, offering a promise of equality. Once he trusts Lucy he is not afraid to reveal to her his vulnerability, to confess that 'there is a fund of modesty and diffidence in my nature' (p. 308), to express that about himself which is tender and nurturing. Finding Lucy asleep at her desk he covers her with a warm shawl and explains to her, when she awakens: 'You need watching, and watching over, and it is well for you that I see this and do my best to discharge both duties' (p. 307). He is not only the 'maitre', the father-lover who haunts all of Brontë's novels. He is also a maternal figure – and, in his stubborn impulsivity and petulance, a child. To Lucy who has had no relationships, he offers all.

Because Monsieur Paul's is such a comprehensive and vital personality, he evokes and even demands a wide range of responses. Although he likes to dominate, his is not an ego which blocks response. His empathetic nature allows him to define himself through interaction. It is revealing that he should feel an affinity with the theatre and choose to direct amateur performances. It is important that he should persuade Lucy to take part in a school production. Her assigned role is one which she despairs at first of playing properly. She is to be a man: Ginevra's suitor, a fop. But she discovers it to be a part that she can not only play well, but can play 'with relish'. Imagining that Graham is her rival, responding to Ginevra's flirtatiousness, to the girl's clear preference for herself, Lucy becomes instinctively the dandy, deHamal, with whom Ginevra eventually elopes. In the process she learns something about each of them and, most importantly, she learns to explore and release some hidden androgynous aspect of her own personality. The knowledge she gains is frightening. The possibility she feels makes her wish to withdraw again into the more limited spaces of herself. 'A keen relish for dramatic expression had revealed itself as part of my nature; to cherish and exercise this new-found faculty might gift me with a world of delight, but it would not do for a mere looker-on at life' (p. 121). Her reaction is composed of the same elements of attraction and repulsion that she experiences when she later goes with Graham to see Vashti, the great actress.[1] In Vashti's performance she finds the very image of passion. She is almost unbearably moved by the 'marvellous sight: a mighty revelation ... a spectacle low, horrible, immoral' (p. 220). Through Vashti is revealed the range of passions available to the human spirit. The actress's power is 'like a deep, swollen winter river, thundering in cataract', which plucks Lucy's soul 'like a leaf, on the steep and steely sweep of its descent' (p. 222). And when the force of Vashti's conflict, the depth of her passion, becomes in fact too much for Lucy to bear, the theatre bursts into flames, much like the mystery of fire which flickers through *Jane Eyre*.

Although Lucy deeply fears such a loss of rational control, she is magnetically drawn by the potential for extension and self-exploration which the irrational seems to hold out to her. Paul Emanuel does not present her with a range of possibilities as vast as those implied by Vashti's performances. These would overwhelm Lucy, as the fire symbolically suggests. He does, however, continue to place her in role-playing situations which prevent her from becoming again 'a mere looker-on at life'. Lucy initially makes the mistake of thinking that Paul Emanuel is simply like all of the others who project upon her roles which express their sense of her and freeze her into false postures:

> Madame Beck esteemed me learned and blue; Miss Fanshawe, caustic, ironic and cynical; Mr. Home, a model teacher, the essence of the sedate and discreet: somewhat conventional perhaps, too strict, limited and scrupulous, but still the pink and pattern of governess-correctness; ...
>
> (p. 257)

In fact, M. Paul can read Lucy's eyes, her face, her gestures – and he responds to the spark of her being instead of the shadow of her seeming. It is a new experience for her, as she observed with some amazement to herself: 'You are well habituated to be passed by as a shadow in Life's sunshine: it is a new thing to see one testily lifting his hand to screen his eyes, because you tease him with an obtrusive ray' (p. 284). Initially, responding to her strength, her 'Protestant independence', Paul sees her as a competitor, 'one of those beings who must be *kept down*' (p. 133). His urge to dominate, inspires her resistance, '[gives] wings to aspiration' (p. 298). His belief that she is more learned than she in fact is and his fear that she will use her learning as a weapon against him, stimulate her confidence. His excessive emotionality (so like her inner self) releases her into perverse playfulness and his mercurial disposition makes her 'placid and harmonious', almost maternal. So too, his jealousy of Graham, which moves him to petulant accusations concerning her 'frivolity' and 'vanity', amuses her while awakening a sense of the power of her own femininity. Asserting herself in opposition to him, Lucy discovers a range of responses, feelings, opinions and ideas which will not be confined to the narrow space of a submerged personality. He sparks her to growth – as Hunsden incites Frances, as Rochester stimulates Jane. But he does not – in the manner of his predecessors – frustrate the spirit he arouses.

As M. Paul becomes aware that Lucy's capacity for passion makes her vulnerable as well as strong, he allows himself to substitute sympathy and support for anger. More secure, he can overcome his suspicions and assure her that 'we worship the same God, in the same spirit, though by different rites' (p. 323). His avowal is not a simple assertion of religious tolerance. It is, in its admission of equality, a genuine offer of friendship: an advance towards psychic confrontation: the beginning for each of emotional fulfilment. To acknowledge religious kinship Paul and Lucy must accept the manifestations of each other in themselves for their religions define the dominant aspects of their personalities. Reason and imagination, control and expression, must be placed in appropriate relationship.

Lucy fears Catholicism because she equates its apparent excesses of feeling with loss of self. She fears it because it offers her, as an alternative to the familiar agony of alienation, the self-contained world of religious fanaticism. She knows that if she had returned to Père Silas after the night of her impulsive confession, 'I might just now, instead of writing this heretic narrative, be counting my beads in a cell of a certain Carmelite convent on the Boulevard of Crecy in Villette' (p. 141). Lucy prefers Art – the rational ordering of intuition and emotion – to the mystical transfiguration which leaves reality behind. But the power of aversion measures the force of attraction.

There is that in Catholicism to which she profoundly responds – both in the sublimity of nature and in the mysticism of her own soul; feelings which represent spiritual and erotic transcendence: the dual temptations of the romantic experience.

For Jane, these feelings were focused in a series of fiery images projected first in the red-room of her childhood; later associated with the vampire, Berthe. Lucy's fear is typically one of deprivation rather than anticipation. It finds its object in the ghostly figure of the nun who haunts her at the Pensionnat. But we are aware of its presence earlier in the novel: when Lucy first begins to confront herself after Miss Marchmont's death. It is then that she unexpectedly meets an old school friend:

> What a beautiful and kind-looking woman was the good-natured and comely, but unintellectual girl become! Wifehood and maternity had changed her thus, as I have seen them change others even less promising than she. Me she had forgotten. I was changed, too; though not, I fear, for the better.
>
> (p. 37)

The girl's life contrasts sharply with the one Lucy has led as nurse to the invalided old woman. Lucy allows herself to feel regret as she looks at the young mother, believing that this kind of transformation will never be hers; that she, Lucy Snowe, can have no hope of wifehood and maternity. And yet – she cannot live contentedly with the certainty of that impossibility.

Later, at the Pensionnat, as she cares for Madame's children, to whom she is 'only a governess', she does often seem (as the billet-doux intended for Ginevra describes her) 'revêche comme une religieuse' (p. 95). It is understandable that she would identify with the nun who is said to haunt the house, the ghost of a girl who had been buried alive 'for some sin against her vow' (p. 90). Lucy has also been 'buried alive', and the spectre is the dread shape of the imprisoned, undeserving self of the past: the sterile and isolated self of the future. The chill form of enforced virginity hovers prophetically over Lucy, as Berthe – unleashed sensuality – had menaced Jane. Both are the perverse offspring of sexual desire and the repression which results from guilt and fear. Both represent the wish for union and the horror of negation. In aspect, Berthe is the projection of Jane's expectant sexuality which is passionate though fearful. The figure of the nun expresses Lucy's only nascent sexuality, anticipatory of rejection and sterility.

When Lucy reads Graham's first letter, her intense joy is countered by terror at the depth of her own happiness: a fear of risk, a resurgence of insecurity. It is then that she first sees the nun. Panicked, she asks: 'Are there wicked things, not human, which envy human bliss?' (p. 210). And when she decides at last to bury Graham's letters – repressing feelings that can only cause her pain – the apparition offers itself again, apparently validating her belief that 'If life be a war, it seemed my destiny to conduct it single-handed' (p. 253).

As Lucy's relationship with Paul begins to flourish, the spectre returns as a warning. But now Paul sees it as well and their kinship is expressed in their shared sensitivity, derived from a surprising similarity of personal history. For him, too, the nun has had a special significance. He associates her with Justine Marie, a young woman who had died in the convent in which she had been placed because of him, by relatives who thought him unsuitable as a lover. The power the girl exerts over him in death creates for Paul a life which is as stunted as the one which the nun seems to prophesy for Lucy. Faithful to Justine's memory, trapped in guilt and sentimentality, Paul has sacrified everything to her family and friends, demonstrating his worthiness repeatedly. To Madame Walravens and Père Silas he has given his energy, his wealth, his hopes for an independent life. He, too, has been a survivor – identifying with the dead. He has lived as a monk, in a space as limited as the one which enclosed Lucy and Miss Marchmont. Now he fears that Justine Marie has come herself, motivated by jealousy of his friendship with Lucy.[2]

The power of the nun is diminished before the secret of her identity is discovered. The Gothic motif is imparted a realism by the psychological validity of Brontë's insight.[3] Because they are functions of human fear, spectres respond to assertions of human will. Superstition is dispelled as Lucy and Paul's belief in one another is substantiated. Learning of Paul's past fidelity and magnanimity, experiencing his tenderness and sympathy, Lucy surrenders to the force of her feeling and to the promise of romance. When they exchange their vow of friendship she believes that she might evade her fate after all: 'I envied no girl her lover, no bride her bridgroom, no wife her husband' (p. 344). Despite his Catholicism, Paul has become for her a 'Christian hero'. He is Apollyon, Great Heart, 'my Champion'.

But although Lucy's happiness seems less threatened by the mysterious forces within, it is threatened still by the jealousy and selfishness of Paul Emanuel's 'friends', as well as by Paul's own fanatic self-sacrifice: his apparent inability to assert himself on behalf of his own needs. Succumbing totally to irrational fear, Lucy perceives Père Silas, Madame Walravens and Madame Beck as the malicious villains of a Gothic tale in which she and Paul are cast as helpless victims. It is in the distorting mirror of Lucy's Protestant prejudices that the reader perceives Père Silas, the bigoted, devious priest and Madame Walravens, who is 'Cunegonde, the sorceress! Malevola, the evil fairy' (p. 329). But if the colours Lucy uses to paint their portraits are lurid, the plan she attributes to them is real. With Madame Beck, they do intend to send Paul Emanuel off to the West Indies for three years on a final 'errand of mercy'. There he will be secured from her heretical influence while looking after their material interests. In Madame Beck's jealous opposition to their love, we hear the outrage of Madame Heger,[4] and in Lucy's wordless desperation as she waits for Paul's last visit, in her sense of impotence before feeling, we feel the passion which Brontë had never before expressed so openly. Because Lucy is secure in Paul's feeling for her as Brontë could never have been in M. Heger's, she is finally able to overcome her passivity, confronting her rival and unmasking her ('I saw underneath a being heartless, self-indulgent, and ignoble' [p. 377]).

Madame Beck's attempts to keep Lucy and Paul separated are self-defeating. The drug which she administers to make Lucy sleep sharpens her senses and intensifies her perceptions. It arouses her, moves her to definitive action.[5] Lucy seeks freedom again as she had sought it before, but now she gives herself completely to her quest. It is a holiday evening and everyone she knows has gathered in the spacious park – radiant with moonlight, alive with the promise of celebration. It is a fitting place for her to seek an encounter with Paul, another of the meetings which have taken place in natural settings, in moonlit gardens, in the open air where the limits of the self are expanded: where the soul can aspire and breathe. Once more a solitary voyeur, Lucy is still not lonely. She projects herself into everything around her. She denies nothing, not even, when she sees Graham, that part of her infatuation for him which always remains potentially alive. Now she searches out experience, eagerly pursuing her 'fate'. She is humorous and ironic, purged of bitterness. Even the reality that undercuts the melodrama of her Gothic vision insists upon recognition:

> Hail, Madame Walravens! I think you looked more witchlike than
> ever. And presently the good lady proved that she was indeed no

corpse or ghost, but a harsh and hardy old woman; for, upon some aggravation in the clamorous petition of Desirée Beck to her mother, to go to the kiosk and take sweetmeats, the hunchback suddenly fetched her a resounding rap with her gold-knobbed cane.

There, then, were Madame Walravens, Madame Beck, Père Silas – the whole conjuration, the secret junta. The sight of them thus assembled did me good. I cannot say that I felt weak before them, or abashed, or dismayed. They outnumbered me, and I was worsted and under their feet; but, as yet, I was not dead.

(p. 388)

The most crucial recognition comes in relation to Paul Emanuel. When she sees him there with his goddaughter, whom she believes to be his intended bride, she responds with a degree of intensity she would never have allowed herself before: 'And then – something tore me so cruelly under my shawl, something so dug into my side, a vulture so strong in beak and talon, I must be alone to grapple with it' (p. 395). Her jealousy teaches her the depth of her love. When she returns to her room with the pain and comprehension of that knowledge, she finds once again – the nun. But the self that has penetrated to truth, and the sexual longing which is at last awakened, both disdain the imagination that builds illusion:

Warm from illuminations, and music, and thronging thousands, thoroughly lashed up by a new scourge, I defied spectra. In a moment, without exclamation, I had rushed on the haunted couch; nothing leaped out, or sprang, or stirred; all the movement was mine, so was all the life, the reality, the substance, the force; as my instinct felt.

(pp. 396–7)

In the absurd reality of the nun (a costume disguise for Ginevra's suitor) Lucy recognises the power of the mind to create its own fears and anxieties; its own guilt, even its own prison. She knows that now she can 'handle the veil and dare the dread glance'. Once the harsh demands of her Protestantism are softened, the repressive ban lifted, Lucy's faith can be confirmed and the integrity of her personality preserved.

The final trial and the ultimate victory remain. Anticipating a meeting with Paul before he sails, fearing that it will not, in fact, take place, Lucy is 'pierced deeper than I could endure, made now to feel what defied suppression'. Forced to the centre of her soul, touching the very quick of her nature, Lucy is undefended at last. When they are reunited she, who has never described herself to the reader (unexpectedly coming upon her reflection in a mirror she had seen simply 'a third person in a pink dress and black lace mantle' [p. 179]), she, Lucy Snowe, risks herself totally, asking: '"Ah! I am not pleasant to look at – ? I could not help saying this; the words came unbidden: I never remember the time when I had not a haunting dread of what might be the degree of my outward deficiency; this dread pressed me at the moment with special force."' It is a validation of her transformed self that she requires. Paul does not disappoint her:

> A great softness passed upon his countenance; his violet eyes grew suffused and glistening under their deep Spanish lashes: he started up: 'Let us walk on.'
> 'Do I displease your eyes much?' I took courage to urge: the point had its vital import for me.
> He stopped, and gave me a short, strong answer – an answer which silenced, subdued, yet profoundly satisfied. Ever after that, I knew what I was for *him*; and what I might be for the rest of the world, I ceased painfully to care.
>
> (p. 407)

With Paul she, who has always found it so difficult to speak, becomes eloquent. She who has hardly dared to tell herself her thoughts, she who has hoarded every feeling, can say, 'I want to tell you all' and she can tell him freely and unbidden of her anxieties and fears. She can tell him also of her love: 'I spoke. All leaped from my lips. I lacked not words now; fast I narrated; fluent I told my tale; it streamed on my tongue' (p. 412). Her capacity for love, newly discovered, newly explored, brings with it self-knowledge and expression.

In his love, Paul has also been able to find the will to self-assertion. He will make this one last journey in Justine Marie's service. Then, returning to marry Lucy, he will commit himself to life. Meanwhile, he plans to make it possible for Lucy to realise her freedom. With the home which he has rented for her and the school which he has established in her name, he offers her the impossible gift of independence. It is the gift which Crimsworth had bestowed upon Frances. But because Lucy must support herself in Paul's absence, because the school is nothing until she creates it, his gift is genuine. Its implications, however, are ambiguous. The role which Paul will play in the school upon his return and the effect which that role will have upon Lucy's functioning: these are not defined. But the novel's conclusion is, in part, an attempt to come to terms with the crucial if unexpressed problems.

When they separate, Paul has demonstrated his sensitivity to Lucy's needs, his generosity in satisfying them. His personality has been softened – the more aggressive and domineering qualities purged. In Lucy's idealised vision, only those elements remain which sustain and nourish. His fidelity is proven. Still, theirs is not a relationship of equality. Lucy sees him as her king: 'royal for me had been that hand's bounty: to offer homage was both a joy and a duty' (p. 410). It is only in his absence that she can and does discover the possibilities of her own strength. Her words are telling: 'M. Emanuel was away three years. Reader, they were the three happiest years of my life' (p. 414). The tone is more telling still. It could be the tone of Jane Eyre. The unreliable narrator has been replaced by one who confronts her reader directly. Lucy Snowe has rejected the silences, the claustrophobic spaces, and the labyrinthian ways of anxiety and repression. She achieves with Brontë herself the maturity of her creator's art. She does not share the totality of Brontë's awareness, however; nor is she allowed the disturbance of her author's subconscious doubts.

Although Lucy can finally assert her independence to become the antithesis of a romantic heroine (neither a 'little spaniel' like Polly nor a thoughtless doll like Ginevra) she is oblivious to the dangers which would confront her if Paul Emanuel should, in fact return. In this novel, as in her three earlier books, it is Brontë who must try to reconcile the heroine's independent self-realisation with her need to be submerged in the powerful, masculine 'other'. For Brontë it had always been impossible to accommodate these two commanding impulses which psychosexual conditioning and social reality place in extreme conflict.

Harriet Martineau, the redoubtable intellectual and social reformer, mistook Charlotte Brontë for Lucy Snowe. With an obtuseness born of militancy, she overlooked the novel's psychological centre and, while noting the resolution of Lucy and Paul Emanuel's relationship, did not mark the significance of the story's ending. In a review which she wrote for the *Daily News*, she evinced the kind of outrage that had typified Mary Taylor's earlier response to *Shirley*:

> All the female characters, in all their thoughts and lives are full of one thing, or are regarded by the reader in the light of one thought – love. It begins with the child of six years old, at the opening – a charming

picture – and it closes with it at the last page; and so dominant is this idea – so incessant is the writer's tendency to describe the need of being loved – that the heroine who tells her own story, leaves the reader at last with the uncomfortable impression of her having either entertained a double love, or allowed one to supersede another without notification of the transition. It is not thus in real life. There are substantial, heartfelt interests for women of all ages and, under ordinary circumstances, quite apart from love; there is an absence of introspection, an unconsciousness, a repose in women's lives – unless under peculiarly unfortunate circumstances – of which we find no admission in this book; and to the absence of it may be attributed some of the criticism which the book will meet with from readers who are no prudes, but whose reason and taste will reject the assumption that events and characters are to be regarded through the medium of one passion only.[6]

Brontë was deeply hurt by the response of this intimidating woman whom she had only just begun to think of as a friend:

I know what *love* is and I understand it; and if man or woman should be ashamed of feeling such love, then there is nothing right, noble, faithful, truthful, unselfish in this earth as I comprehend rectitude, nobleness, fidelity, truth and disinterestedness.[7]

Her words, while naïvely courageous, suggest her continuing inability to break free entirely of that circle of romantic idealism which had bound her life.

Charlotte Brontë had shared Harriet Martineau's feminist outrage when she had intuitively created Elizabeth Hastings, when she had confusedly defined Frances Henri, when she had constructed the mythology of *Jane Eyre* and tested it – unsuccessfully – against the social vision of *Shirley*. But she had never been able to deny what remained for her the most profound of human truths: that to be able to love and to be loved are essential conditions of a maturely realised life. How to reach that loving state, how to treasure it, while still maintaining independence: here was the difficulty. Brontë could offer no clear resolution – witness her elimination of Paul Emanuel – but she would not deny the possibility of resolution altogether. She could only assert the incontrovertible fact of her own situation, revealing in this way the nature and limits of her feminist consciousness. Her personal history had made it impossible for her to draw upon the kind of strengths that had carried Mary Taylor to New Zealand and had allowed Harriet Martineau to create for herself a lifestyle and work defined by radical action and social service. Brontë had neither the self-confidence nor the militance to leave behind the conventional patterns of her world. Her freedom was private and subjective, conceived neither in political nor collective terms. Her feminism derived from her persistent attempt to define herself autonomously, resisting predetermined cultural formulations, responding to the powerful demands of her own personality. Knowledge and growth were garnered from the metaphor of Yorkshire nature and the revelations of introspection. And, of course, for her action was the process of writing.

As she struggled with herself to bring her novel to conclusion, Brontë wrote to George Smith:

> If Lucy marries anybody, it must be the Professor – a man in whom there is much to forgive, much to 'put up with'. But I am not leniently disposed to Miss Frost: from the beginning I never meant to appoint her lines in pleasant places. The conclusion of this third volume is still a matter of some anxiety: I can but do my best, however. It would speedily be finished, could I ward off certain obnoxious head-aches which, whenever I get into the spirit of my work are apt to seize and prostrate me.[8]

The words suggest that Brontë paid to the end the price of personal confrontation. She could not appoint Lucy Snowe's lines in pleasant places because she could not bury again the self which she had so painfully uncovered. Therefore, she could not resolve the conundrum raised by Lucy's situation with the illusions, evasiveness and facility of the earlier novels.

Paul Emanuel could not return. He could not return because Brontë's fantasy relationship with Heger would not then have been laid to rest. The Belgian's idealisation would not have been balanced by his irrevocable loss. The tragic circumstances of her life would have been denied. No matter how great her desire and how firm her wish to believe, no matter how unprepared she was to confront directly the irreducible fact of Heger's indifference, Brontë could not betray the larger reality of her experience.

Then, too, Paul Emanuel could not return for a reason which Martineau would have found congenial had she been able to perceive it through her rigidly structured feminism. Always intensely personal in her writing – faithful to the truths she had learned and to the confusions which remained – Brontë knew that Lucy had come to her independence through love. She understood that for Lucy to be certain of keeping that independence, she would have to pay the price of solitude. Brontë could not be sure that there was in fact another alternative. She did not know what would happen to that emergent self if it were joined in marriage to 'a man in whom there is much to forgive, much to "put up with"'; if it were joined in marriage, in fact, to any man. Her own marriage might have taught her the answer and the answer might well have provided her with another novel. Now she eschewed the former compromises of myth and fantasy.

Paul Emanuel's death *can* be compared to the symbolic castration of Rochester. It too represents a rejection of patriarchal forces and suggests the personal and imaginative losses which result from social failure. But Paul Emanuel cannot be reborn, as Rochester was, into a new version of psychosexual romance. Romance itself is no longer viable. It belongs to the realm of princes and princesses of Fortune: the Graham Brettons and Pauline Homeses. For Lucy Snowe, the conventions of literary form – the shroud of domesticity and the implied perpetuation of social values – are as inadequate as the social conventions which call them into being.

Lucy speaks often of lives which are blessed, of love which ends in happiness and marriage, but when she does, she refers always to the relationship between Polly and Graham and theirs is not a relationship which she herself could value. This much she had revealed to Polly:

> I shall share no man's or woman's life in this world, as you understand sharing. I think I have one friend of my own, but I am not sure; and till I *am* sure, I live solitary.

To Polly's response, 'But solitude is sadness', Lucy adds, 'Yes; it is sadness. Life, however, has worse than that. Deeper than melancholy, lies heartbreak' (p. 359). Because Lucy – like Miss Marchmont – has loved and been loved, the harshness of her 'fate' has been softened. She need not know heartbreak, only sadness. After Paul's death, she receives at last the inheritance from Miss Marchmont. She is responsible for her school. She is of use. She pursues her talents and maintains relationships. Without hope, she is not happy, but she is strong. Virginal, she has still experienced passion. Childless, her life is full of children and will not be sterile. Alone and lonely, she is not alienated. Surviving, she need not live as a survivor. She does not have to tell the story of another. Now she can tell and understand her own.

Paul Emanuel dies at sea as he journeys home. The storm in which he perishes limns the paradox at the novel's centre. It expresses as well the struggle at the heart of the romantic experience and the irony of Brontë's life and death. The expanded self is poised between knowledge and annihilation. The self that is limited and withdrawn neither risks the second nor achieves the first. For Lucy the storm has always had a double meaning. Sometimes it has brought the horror of suffocation. At other times, it has stood for explosive transcendence. Always it has involved a terrible risk. Now Lucy's growth rests – with Brontë's integrity – upon the awful inevitability of Paul's loss. It is an uncompromising vision, but within the context of this novel, which gathers together the threads of all the fictions and the fragments of the life itself, it is undeniable and right.

From Helene Moglen, *Charlotte Brontë: The Self Conceived* (New York, 1976), pp. 214–29.

NOTES

[This excerpt is taken from Helene Moglen's critical biography which provided one of the first extended feminist analyses of Charlotte Brontë and her work. It proceeds on the assumption that there is a direct relationship between life and literature both for the author and for the reader. Thus, Moglen contends that Brontë's novels illuminate her life, arguing, for example, that *Villette* can be read as Brontë's therapeutic confrontation with loneliness. Similarly, she believes that Brontë's life and work offer the reader insights into the modern female psyche and the feminist struggle. Moglen's conviction that the romantic impulse, and particularly the Byronic influence, provided a shaping focus in Brontë's life accounts for the psychosexual focus of her study and for the stress on the figure of M. Paul in the excerpt reprinted here. All quotations in the essay are taken from *Villette* (Boston: Houghton-Mifflin, 1971). Ed.]

1. This incident is modelled on Charlotte Brontë's experience with the French tragedienne, Rachel (Elisa Felix), whom she saw in Scribe's *Adrienne Lecouvreur* and Corneille's *Les Trois Horaces* in London, in June 1851. She wrote to James Taylor of her response (15 November, 1851. *The Brontë's: Their Lives, Friendships and Correspondence*, ed. T. J. Wise and J. A. Symington [Oxford, 1932], vol. 3, p. 289):

   Rachel's acting transfixed me with wonder, enchained me with interest, and thrilled me with horror. The tremendous force with which she expresses the very worst passions in their strongest essence forms an exhibition as exciting as the bull-fights of Spain and the gladiatorial combats of old Rome, and (it seemed to me) not one whit more moral than those poisoned stimulants to popular ferocity. It is scarcely human nature that she shows you; it is something wilder and worse; the feelings and fury of a fiend.

She also wrote:

I neither love, esteem, nor hate this strange being, but (if I could bear the high mental stimulus so long) I would go every night for three months to watch and study its manifestations. (David Isenberg, 'Charlotte Brontë and the Theatre', in *Brontë Society Transactions*, 15:3 [1968], 239).

2. One must remember that Heger was also a survivor, who witnessed the deaths of his first wife and child. By metaphorically developing this aspect of his experience, Brontë undercuts the importance of his second marriage – and second family.

3. For a useful discussion of Charlotte Brontë's adaptation of Gothic forms and technique to psychological purposes, see Robert B. Heilman, 'Charlotte Brontë's New Gothic', in *From Jane Austen to Joseph Conrad*, ed. Robert C. Rathburn and Martin Steinmann, Jr (Minnesota, 1958), pp. 118–32.

4. Writing to Ellen of Madame Heger's coldness towards her, Charlotte comes as close as she did in any of her existing letters to sharing her secret infatuation (15 November, 1843. *The Brontë's: Their Lives, Friendships and Correspondence*, ed. T. J. Wise and J. A. Symington [Oxford, 1932] vol. 2, p. 309):

You will hardly believe that Madame Heger (good and kind as I have described her) never comes near me on the occasions. . . . I own, I was astonished the first time I was left alone thus . . . you remember the letter she wrote me when I was in England? How kind and affectionate that was! is it not odd? I fancy I begin to perceive the reason of this mighty distance and reserve; it sometimes makes me laugh and at other times nearly cry. When I am sure of it I will tell you.

5. Elizabeth Gaskell writes (Gaskell, *The Life of Charlotte Brontë* [1857; reprinted London, 1974], chap. xxvii):

I asked her whether she had ever taken opium, as the description given of its effects in *Villette* was so exactly like what I had experienced, – vivid and exaggerated presence of objects, of which the outlines were indistinct, or lost in golden mist, etc. She replied, that she had never, to her knowledge, taken a grain of it in any shape, but that she had followed the process she had always adopted when she had to describe anything which had not fallen within her own experience; she had thought intently on it for many and many a night before falling to sleep, – wondering what it was like, or how it would be, – till at length, sometimes after the progress of her story had been arrested at this one point for weeks, she wakened up in the morning with all clear before her, as if she had in reality gone through the experience, and then could describe it, word for word, as it happened.

6. T. J. Wise and J. A. Symington (eds), *The Brontës: Their Lives, Friendships and Correspondence* (London, 1932), vol. 4, p. 44.

7. To Harriet Martineau, January 1853. Ibid., vol. 4, p. 42.

8. 3 November, 1852. Ibid., vol. 4, p. 16.

2

Sexual Politics in 'Villette'

KATE MILLETT

Lucy Snowe, the heroine of Charlotte Brontë's *Villette*,[1] a book too subversive to be popular, is another matter. In Lucy one may perceive what effects her life in a male-supremacist society has upon the psyche of a woman. She is bitter and she is honest; a neurotic revolutionary full of conflict, back-sliding, anger, terrible self-doubt, and an unconquerable determination to win through. She is a pair of eyes watching society; weighing, ridiculing, judging. A piece of furniture whom no one notices, Lucy sees everything and reports, cynically, compassionately, truthfully, analytically. She is no one, because she lacks any trait that might render her visible: beauty, money, conformity. Only a superb mind imperfectly developed and a soul so omnivorously large it casts every other character into the shadows, she is the great exception, the rest only the great mediocre rule.

Lucy is a woman who has watched men and can tell you what they are as seen by the woman they fail to notice. Some are like John Graham Bretton, charming egoists. Their beauty, for Brontë is perhaps the first woman who ever admitted in print that women find men beautiful, amazes and hurts her. Bretton is two people: one is Graham the treasured and privileged man-child seen through the eyes of a slighted sister, whether the distant idolator be Lucy or Missy Home. Brontë keeps breaking people into two parts so we can see their divided and conflicting emotions; Missy is the worshipful sister, Lucy the envious one. Together they represent the situation of the girl in the family. Bretton is both the spoiled son Graham, and the successful doctor John, and in both roles Lucy envies, loves and hates him. Never does the situation permit her to love him in peace, nor him to take notice of her in any but the most tepid and patronising good humour: sterile, indifferent. His beauty and goodness make him lovable; his privilege and egotism make him hateful. The enormous deprivation of her existence causes Lucy to resemble a ghetto child peering up at a Harvard man – envy, admiration, resentment and dislike; yet with a tremendous urge to love – if it were possible to love one so removed, so diffident, so oppressive, so rich, disdainful and unjustly superior in place.

If the male is not the delightful and infuriating egoist whom maturity means learning to relinquish one's 'crush' on, he is the male one encounters a bit later in life when one tries to make one's way. He is Paul Emanuel, the voice of piety, conventionality, male supremacy, callow chauvinism terrified of female 'competition'. John is unconquerable; he will never acknowledge any woman who is not beautiful or rich, his only qualifications; he loved Fanshaw's stupidity just as readily as Paulina Mary's virtue. Women are decorative objects to him. Paul is easier to cope with; in his sexual antagonism there is something more tractable. John Graham never saw Lucy; Paul sees her and hates her. Here it is possible to establish contact and, as the story is all a fantasy of success (a type of success utterly impossible to achieve in Brontë's period, and so necessarily fantastic) Paul is met and persuaded. To his sneer that she is ignorant and women are dolts, Lucy replies with phenomenal intellectual effort. Despite the impossible atmosphere he gives off as a pedagogue, the bullying, the captivity in overheated rooms, the endless spying, the bowdlerising of her texts – she learns. It is his ridicule that forces her to achieve, pokes her into development, deprives her of the somnolence of ladyhood, its small ambitions, timidity and self-doubt.

Lucy watches women – again from a double and even more complicated point of vantage. She studies Ginevra Fanshawe the flirt, an idiot beauty callously using men to acquire what she has been carefully taught to want: admiration, money, the petty power of dominating a puppy. Fanshawe is beautiful too, and Lucy, in every respect the product of her society as well as its enemy and rebel, has been schooled to love this beauty. It stirs her. The book is full of references to the desire such beauty arouses in her. To express it, Brontë invents the device of an afternoon of amateur theatrics. Lucy is dragged into them at the last moment to play Fanshawe's lover. It is another of Paul's bullying schemes (he locks her in an attic in the July heat to be sure she learns her lines) to coerce her into courage and achievement. Lucy succeeds miraculously, and she makes love to Fanshawe on stage in one of the most indecorous scenes one may come upon in the entire Victorian novel. (Brontë is too much an insurrectionary to acknowledge any convention beyond the literary and the most astonishing things occur continuously in her fiction.) Just as maturity and success lie in outgrowing an infatuation with Graham's masculine egotism, or Paul's bullying but productive chauvinism, they are also a matter of renouncing a masculine lust for Fanshawe. She is too dumb to love, too silly to want or to permit oneself to be wounded by. The dialogue between the two young women is brutal; Fanshawe parades her beauty with the double purpose of making Lucy capitulate before it, acknowledge herself an ugly woman and therefore inferior; or propose herself a suitor to it and therefore a captive through desire. For Ginevra knows critical Lucy would be the best catch of all, the biggest conquest. Lucy holds her own in these cruel sessions and won't be had either way. Ultimately, she transcends them and Fanshawe altogether, who fades into the mere butterfly she is and disappears from the book.

The other women Lucy watches are Madame Beck and Mrs Bretton. Both are older women, one a mother, one a businesswoman and head of a school. They are two of the most efficient women one can meet anywhere in fiction. Lucy, who, like Charlotte Brontë, lacked a mother, regards older women as the embodiment of competence, and what she loves in them is their brilliant ability to manage. While Victorian masculine fantasy saw only tender, quivering incapacity in such women, Lucy perceives them as big, capable ships and herself only a little boat. But the big ships are afloat because they knew how to compromise; Lucy does not plan to. The big ships are convention. For all the playful banter of her relationship with her son, Mrs Bretton stands for a stale and selfless maternity, bent on living vicariously through her adored boy's success. Pleasant matron that she is, she would sacrifice any daughter in the world for the comfort of his lordly breakfast, and Lucy knows it. Mrs Bretton's conventional motherhood is only the warm perfection of chauvinist sentiment. Then there is Madame Beck, a tower of convention, the tireless functionary of European sexual inhibition, watching every move of the young women under her Jehovah-like and unsleeping surveillance; getting up at night to examine Lucy's underwear, reading her letters to sniff out traces of sex in them, watching for missives thrown from windows to her pupils. Both these women are still young and ripe for sexuality. Mrs Bretton fulfils her own in flirtation with her son:

> 'Mamma, I'm in a dangerous way.'
> 'As if that interested me,' said Mrs Bretton.
> 'Alas! the cruelty of my lot!' responded her son. 'Never man had a more unsentimental mother than mine; she never seems to think that such a calamity can befall her as a daughter-in-law.'
> 'If I don't, it is not for want of having that same calamity held over my head; you have threatened me with it for the last ten years. "Mamma, I am going to be married soon!" was the cry before you were well out of jackets.'
> 'But mother, one of these days it will be realized. All of a sudden, when you think you are most secure, I shall go forth like Jacob or Esau, or any other patriarch, and take me a wife, perhaps of these which are of the daughters of the land.'
> 'At your peril, John Graham! that is all.'[2]

Beck is more sensually alive and would be delighted to take on John Graham, but of course she is not sufficiently young, beautiful, or socially prominent for his tastes. Real as her own sexuality is, she will gracefully acknowledge his rejection, and serenely carry on the business, while cheerfully stamping out the intrusion of the least hint of sex in any corner of her establishment. As the educator of young females, Madame Beck is a perpetual policewoman, a virtual forewoman of patriarchal society. No system of subjection could operate for two seconds without its collaborators, and Beck is a splendid example of the breed.

Finally, there is Paulina Mary, the golden one, the perfect woman, John Graham's pretty Polly, the apple of her daddy's eye. Lucy had no father to dote upon her, nor any John to court her, and she is painfully aware that Paulina is lucky. Yet there is one flaw in this female paragon – she is a child of eight – delightful when she appears as Missy Home at the beginning of the book; clever, affectionate, precocious – but nauseating when she reappears as a woman of nineteen and still a mental infant. Paulina is well-meaning and well loved. Even Lucy is fond of her from time to time, but she is also appalled that society's perfect woman must be a cute pre-adolescent. Having surveyed the lot, Lucy prefers to be like none of them. Looking over all the 'role models' her world presents, the adoring mother, the efficient prison matron, the merciless flirt, the baby-goddess, Lucy, whose most genuine trial is that she has been born into a world where there are no adequate figures to imitate so that she is forced to grope her way alone, a pioneer without precedents, turns her back on the bunch of them. Better to go back to something solidly her own – deal with mathematics, Paul Emanuel, and the job. Lucy has watched men look at women, has studied the image of woman in her culture. There is probably nothing so subversive in the book as that afternoon in the Brussels museum when she scrutinises the two faces of woman whom the male has fashioned, one for his entertainment, one for her instruction: Rubens' Cleopatra and the Academician's four pictures of the virtuous female. Lucy's deliberately philistine account of Cleopatra is very entertaining:

> It represented a woman, considerably larger, I thought, than the life. I calculated that this lady, put into a scale of magnitude suitable for the reception of a commodity of bulk, would infallibly turn from fourteen to sixteen stones. She was indeed extremely well fed. Very much butchers' meat, to say nothing of bread, vegetables, and liquids, must she have consumed to attain that breadth and height, that wealth of muscle, that affluence of flesh. She lay half-reclined on a couch, why, it would be difficult to say; broad daylight blazed round her; she appeared in hearty health, strong enough to do the work of two plain cooks; she could not plead a weak spine; she ought to have been standing, or at least sitting bolt upright. She had no business to lounge away the noon on a sofa.... Then, for the wretched untidiness surrounding her, there could be no excuse. Pots and pans, perhaps I ought to say vases and goblets, were rolled here and there on the foreground; a perfect rubbish of flowers was mixed amongst them, and an absurd and disorderly mass of certain upholstery smothered the couch, and cumbered the floor.[3]

This 'coarse and preposterous canvas', this 'enormous piece of claptrap', as Lucy nominates the masturbatory fantasy she perceives in it, is the male dream of an open and panting odalisque, the sheer carnality floating always in the back of his mind, and can be matched only by its obverse – the image of woman he would foist on the woman herself. Cleopatra is for masculine delectation only, and when Paul catches Lucy contemplating the painting he is deeply shocked: 'How dare you, a young person, sit coolly down, with the self-possession of a garçon, and look at *that* picture?'[4] A despot, as Lucy describes him so often, he is deeply offended, even affronted, that a young woman should see what he immediately settles down to gaze at. Paul forbids Lucy to look upon Cleopatra, and forces her to sit in a dull corner and study several mawkish daubs the conventional mind has designed for her:

a set of four, denominated in the catalogue, 'La vie d' une femme'. They were painted in a remarkable style, flat, dead, pale and formal. The first represented a 'Jeune fille', coming out of a church door, a missal in her hand, her dress very prim, her eyes cast down, her mouth pursed up – the image of a most villainous, little, precocious she-hypocrite. The second, a 'Mariée' with a long white veil, kneeling at a prie-dieu in her chamber, holding her hands plastered together, finger to finger, and showing the whites of her eyes in the most exasperating manner. The third, a 'Jeune Mère' hanging disconsolate over a clayey and puffy baby with a face like an unwholesome full moon. The fourth, a 'Veuve', being a black woman, holding by the hand a black little girl [black because in mourning] and the twain studiously surveying an elegant French monument.... All these four 'Anges' were grim and grey as burglars, and cold and vapid as ghosts. What women to live with! insecure, ill-humoured, bloodless, brainless nonentities! As bad in their way as the indolent gipsy giantess, the Cleopatra, in hers.[5]

In this comic instance of sight taboo, the social schizophrenia within masculine culture, not only the hypocrisy of the double standard, but its purpose and intentions are exposed. It has converted one woman into sex symbol, flesh devoid of mentality or personality, 'cunt' – this for itself to gaze upon. And unto woman herself is reserved the wearisome piety of academic icons with their frank propaganda of serviceable humility.

The disparity in the contradiction of images represented by the two pictures explains the techniques of *Villette* better than any other moment in the novel. It is a division in the culture which Brontë is retorting to by splitting her people in half and dividing Lucy's own responses into a fluctuating negative and positive. The other dichotomy is between her newness, her revolutionary spirit, and the residue of the old ways which infects her soul. This inner conflict is complemented by an exterior one between her ambitions and desires and the near impossibility of their fulfilment. There are obstacles everywhere, social and financial. The hard realities of the sexual caste system frustrate her as well as its mentality. Curiously enough, the obstacles drive her on. Lucy represents not only Brontë's, but what must have been, and probably still remains, the ambition of every conscious young woman in the world. She wants to be free; she is mad to escape, to learn, to work, to go places. She envies every man his occupation, John his medicine, Paul his scholarship, just as she envied them their education. Both had the finest obtainable and it was given to them as a preparation for life. Lucy was given nothing so substantial:

picture me for the next eight years, as a bark slumbering through halycon weather, in a harbour as still as glass – the steersman stretched on the little deck, his face up to heaven, his eyes closed. . . . A great many women and girls are supposed to pass their lives something in that fashion; why not I with the rest? . . . However, it cannot be concealed that in that case, I must somehow have fallen overboard, or there must have been a wreck at last.[6]

She is traumatically cast out of the middle class quite unprepared to live, for all the world had expected her to exist parasitically. She now lacks the prerequisites: a face, respectable social connections, and parents to place her. She is a serf without a proprietor who must become a wage slave, namely a governess or teacher. The only way out, and it's a desperate track, is to learn the world and books. *Villette* chronicles her formal and informal education in the acquisition of her own competence through both.

But what work can Lucy do; what occupations are open to her? Paid companion, infant nurse, governess, schoolteacher. As they are arranged, each is but another name for servant. Each involves starvation wages which only a lifetime of saving could ever convert to ransom. There is another humiliation in the fact of servant status which rested with particular severity on middle-class women who in taking employment are falling a step below the class of their birth. (While a paid companion, Lucy encounters a schoolmate now the mistress of a household – Lucy had been visiting another servant in the kitchen.) Furthermore, these occupations involve 'living-in' and a twenty-four-hour surveillance tantamount to imprisonment. The only circumstances under which Lucy is permitted an occupation are such that they make financial independence and personal fulfilment impossible. It is not very hard to understand her envy at the gratification and status which Paul and John are given automatically in their professions. One might well ask, as Lucy does unceasingly, is it worth it then, under these conditions, to work? Is it not easier to keep falling into daydreams about prince charmings who will elevate one to royalty, or so they claim? At any rate, they could provide easy security and a social position cheaply attained. They will provide, if nothing else, the sexual gratification which women occupied like Lucy are utterly forbidden to enjoy.

Villette reads, at times, like another debate between the opposed mentalities of Ruskin and Mill. Lucy is forever alternating between hankering after the sugared hopes of chivalric rescue, and the strenuous realism of Mill's analysis. Brontë demonstrates thereby that she knows what she is about. In her circumstances, Lucy would not be creditable if she were not continuously about to surrender to convention; if she were not by turns silly as well as sensible. So there are many moments when she wishes she were as pretty as Fanshawe, as rich as Polly, occasions when she would happily forgo life itself at a sign that Graham recognises she was alive. Born to a situation where she is subject to life-and-death judgements based on artificial standards of beauty, Lucy is subject to a compulsive mirror obsession, whereby each time she looks in the glass she denies her existence – she does not appear in the mirror. One of the most interesting cases of inferiority feelings in literature, Lucy despises her exterior self, and can build an inner being only through self-hatred. Yet living in a culture which takes masochism to be a normal phenomenon in females, and even conditions them to enjoy it, Lucy faces and conquers the attractions Paul's sadism might have held.

Charlotte Brontë has her public censor as well as her private one to deal with. This accounts for the deviousness of her fictional devices, her continual flirtation with the bogs of sentimentality which period feeling mandates she sink in though she be damned if she will. Every Victorian novel is expected to end in a happy marriage; those written by women are required to. Brontë pretends to compromise; convention is appeased by the pasteboard wedding of Paulina Mary and Prince John; cheated in Lucy's escape.

Escape is all over the book; *Villette* reads like one long meditation on a prison break. Lucy will not marry Paul even after the tyrant has softened. He has been her jailer all through the novel, but the sly and crafty captive in Lucy is bent on evading him anyway. She plays tame, learns all he has to teach her of the secrets of the establishment – its mathematics and Latin and self-confidence. She plays pupil to a man who hates and fears intelligent women and boasts of having caused the only woman teacher whose learning ever challenged his own to lose her job. Lucy endures the baiting about the 'natural inferiority of females' with which Paul tortures her all through the lesson, and understands that only the outer surface of his bigotry melts when she proves a good student and thereby flatters his pedagogic vanity. Yet in his simplicity he has been hoodwinked into giving her the keys. The moment they are in her hand, and she has beguiled him into lending her money, renting her a school of her own, and facilitated her daring in slipping from the claws of Madame Beck – she's gone. The keeper turned kind must be eluded anyway; Paul turned lover is drowned.

Lucy is free. Free is alone; given a choice between 'love' in its most agreeable contemporary manifestation, and freedom, Lucy chose to retain the individualist humanity she had shored up, even at the expense of sexuality. The sentimental reader is also free to call Lucy 'warped', but Charlotte Brontë is hard-minded enough to know that there was no man in Lucy's society with whom she could have lived and still been free. On those occasions when Brontë did marry off her heroines, the happy end is so fraudulent, the marriages so hollow, they read like satire, or cynical tracts against love itself. There was, in Lucy's position, just as in the Brontë's own, no other solution available. As there is no remedy to sexual politics in marriage, Lucy very logically doesn't marry. But it is also impossible for a Victorian novel to recommend a woman not marry. So Paul suffers a quiet sea burial. Had Brontë's heroine 'adjusted' herself to society, compromised, and gone under, we should never have heard from her. Had Brontë herself not grown up in a house of half-mad sisters with a domestic tyrant for father, no 'prospects', as marital security was referred to, and with only the confines of governessing and celibacy staring at her from the future, her chief release the group fantasy of 'Angria', that collective dream these strange siblings played all their lives, composing stories about a never-never land where women could rule, exercise power, govern the state, declare night and day, death and life – then we would never have heard from Charlotte either.[7] Had that been the case, we might never have known what a resurrected soul wished to tell upon emerging from several millennia of subordination. Literary criticism of the Brontë's has been a long game of masculine prejudice wherein the player either proves they can't write and are hopeless primitives, whereupon the critic sets himself up like a schoolmaster to edit their stuff and point out where they went wrong, or converts them into case histories from the wilds, occasionally prefacing his moves with a few pseudo-sympathetic remarks about the windy house on the moors, or old maidhood, following with an attack on every truth the novels contain, waged by anxious pedants who fear Charlotte might 'castrate' them or Emily 'unman' them with her passion. There is bitterness and anger in *Villette* – and rightly so. One finds a good deal of it in Richard Wright's *Black Boy*, too. To label it neurotic is to mistake symptom for cause in the hope of protecting oneself from what could be upsetting.

What should surprise us is not Lucy's wry annoyance, but her affection and compassion – even her wit. *Villette* is one of the wittier novels in English and one of the rare witty books in an age which specialised in sentimental comedy. What is most satisfying of all is the astonishing degree of consciousness one finds in the work, the justice of its analysis, the fairness of its observations, the generous degree of self-criticism. Although ocasionally flawed with mawkish nonsense (there is a creditable amount of Victorian syrup in *Villette*), it is nevertheless one of the most interesting books of the period and, as an expression of revolutionary sensibility, a work of some importance.

From Kate Millett, *Sexual Politics* (New York, 1970), pp. 140–7.

NOTES

[This excerpt is taken from one of the central texts of early feminism. Like Mary Ellmann's *Thinking About Women* (New York, 1968) and Germaine Greer's *The Female Eunuch* (London, 1970), Millett's study insisted upon the essentially political nature of sexual relations and of representation. While the passage excerpted brilliantly opened up a feminist reading of *Villette*, it is not typical of the literary analysis in the book which focuses not on women writers, but on the sexist representation of male writers such as D. H. Lawrence, Henry Miller and Norman Mailer. Millett's general thesis has been criticised by later feminists as overly simplistic in its conception of ideology as monolithic (see Toril Moi, *Sexual/Textual Politics* [London, 1985]) and her reading of *Villette* has been challenged for failing to take account of the novel's inconsistencies and of its non-realist aspect (see Mary Jacobus, p. 121 below). Ed.]

1. Charlotte Brontë, *Villette*, first published in 1853 under the pseudonym Currer Bell. Reprinted by the Gresham Publishing Company, London, undated. Page numbers refer to this edition. Throughout my remarks I am indebted to an unpublished essay on Charlotte Brontë's *Shirley* written by Laurie Stone.

2. Ibid., p. 193.

3. Ibid., p. 183.

4. Ibid., p. 184.

5. Ibid., p. 185.

6. Ibid., p. 32.

7. See Fannie Ratchford, *The Brontës' Web of Childhood* (New York, 1941).

3

The Buried Life of Lucy Snowe

SANDRA M. GILBERT and SUSAN GUBAR

It is amazing . . . how mysterious Lucy's complaint remains. Indeed, unless one interprets backwards from the breakdown, it is almost incomprehensible: Lucy's conflicts are hidden because, as we have seen, she represents them through the activity of other people. As self-effacing a narrator as she is a character, she often seems to be telling any story but her own. Polly Home, Miss Marchmont, Madame Beck and Ginevra are each presented in more detail, with more analysis, than Lucy herself. The resulting obscurity means that generations of readers have assumed Brontë did not realise her subject until she was half-finished with the book. It means, too, that the work's mythic elements, although recognised, have been generally misunderstood or rejected as unjustifiable. And, after all, why should Lucy's schizophrenia be viewed as a generic problem facing all women? It is this question, with all that it implies, that Brontë confronts in the interlude at the centre of *Villette*.

We have already seen that, in telling the stories of other women, Lucy is telling her own tale with as much evasion and revelation as Brontë is in recounting her personal experiences through the history of Lucy Snowe. Just as Brontë alters her past in order to reveal it, Lucy's ambivalence about her 'heretic narrative' (ch. 15) causes her to leave much unsaid. Certainly there is a notable lack of specificity in her account. The terrors of her childhood, the loss of her parents, the unreturned love she feels for Dr John, and the dread of her nightmares during the long vacation are recounted in a curiously allusive way. Instead of describing the actual events, for instance, Lucy frequently uses water imagery to express her feelings of anguish at these moments of suffering. Her turbulent childhood is a time of briny waves when finally 'the ship was lost, the crew perished' (ch. 4); Dr John's indifference makes her feel like 'the rock struck, and Meribah's waters gushing out' (ch. 13); during the long vacation, she sickens because of tempestuous and wet weather bringing a dream that forces to her lips a black, strong, strange drink drawn from the boundless sea (ch. 15). This imagery is especially difficult because water is simultaneously associated with security. For example, Lucy remembers her visits to the Brettons as peaceful intervals, like 'the sojourn of Christian and Hopeful beside a certain pleasant stream' (ch. 1). This last life-giving aspect of water is nowhere more apparent than in Lucy's return to consciousness after her headlong pitch down the abyss. At this point she discovers herself in the Bretton home, now miraculously placed just outside the city of Villette. Taking in the blue-green room of La Terrasse, she feels reborn into the comfort of a deep submarine chamber. When she has reached this safe asylum (complete with wonderful tea, seedcake, and godmother), she can only pray to be content with a temperate draught of the living stream.

Although she is now willing to drink, however, she continues to fear that once she succumbs to her thirst she will apply too passionately to the welcome waters. Nevertheless, Lucy is given a second chance: she is reborn into the same conflict, but with the realisation that she cannot allow herself to die of thirst. As in her earlier novels, Brontë traces the woman's revolt against paternalism in her heroine's ambivalence about God the Father. Jane Eyre faced the overwhelming 'currents' of St John *Rivers*' enthusiasm which threatened to destroy her as much as the total absence of faith implied by the unredemptive role of *Grace/Poole*. In *Villette*, Lucy Snowe wants to believe that 'the waiting waters will stir for the cripple and the blind, the dumb and the possessed' who 'will be led to bathe' (ch. 17). Yet, she knows that 'Thousands lie round the pool, weeping and despairing, to see it through slow years, stagnant' (ch. 17). If the waters stir, what do they bring? Do the weeping and despairing wait for death or resurrection? Drowning or baptism? Immersion or engulfment? Lucy never departs from the subjunctive or imperative or interrogative when discussing the redemption to come, because her desire for such salvation is always expressed as a hope and a prayer, never as a belief. Aware that life on earth is based on an inequality, which has presumably been countenanced by a power greater than herself, she sardonically, almost sarcastically, admits that His will shall be done, 'whether we humble ourselves to resignation or not' (ch. 38).

The very problematic quality of the water imagery, then, reflects Lucy's ambivalence. It is as confusing as it is illuminating, as much a camouflage as a disclosure. Her fear of role-playing quite understandably qualifies the way she speaks or writes, and her reticence as a narrator makes her especially unreliable when she deals with what she most fears. To the consternation of many critics who have bemoaned her trickery,[1] not only does she withhold Dr John's last name from the reader, she never divulges the contents of his letters, and, until the end of her story, she persistently disclaims warm feelings for him. Furthermore, she consistently withholds information from other characters out of mere perversity. She never, for instance, voluntarily tells Dr John that he helped her on the night of her arrival in Villette, or that she remembers him as Graham from Bretton days; later, when she recounts an evening at a concert to Ginevra, she falsifies the account; and even when she wishes to tell M. Paul that she has heard his story, she mockingly reverses what she has learned. Indeed, although Lucy is silent in many scenes, when she does speak out, her voice retreats from the perils of self-definition behind sarcasm and irony. 'But if I feel, may I *never* express?' she asks herself, only to hear her reason declare, 'Never!' (ch. 21). Even in the garden, she can only parody Ginevra and Dr John (chs 14–15), and when her meaning is misunderstood on any of these occasions, she takes 'pleasure in thinking of the contrast between reality and [her] description' (ch. 21).

Why would Brontë choose a narrator who purposefully tries to evade the issues or mislead the reader? This is what Lucy seems to do when she allows the reader to picture her childhood 'as a bark slumbering through halcyon weather' because 'A great many women and girls are supposed to pass their lives something in this fashion' (ch. 4). Why does Brontë choose a voyeur to narrate a fictional biography when this means that the narrator insists on telling the tale as if some other, more attractive woman were its central character? Obviously, Lucy's life, her sense of herself, does not conform to the literary or social stereotypes provided by her culture to define and circumscribe female life. Resembling Goethe's Makarie in that she too feels as if she has no story, Lucy cannot employ the narrative structures available to her, yet there are no existing alternatives. So she finds herself using and abusing – presenting and undercutting – images and stories of male devising, even as she omits or elides what has been deemed unsuitable, improper, or aberrant in her own experience.

That Lucy feels anxious and guilty about her narrative is evident when she wonders whether an account of her misfortunates might not merely disturb others, whether the half-drowned life-boatman shouldn't keep his own counsel and spin no yarns (ch. 17). At more than one point in her life, she considers it wise, for those who have experienced inner turmoil or madness in solitary confinement, to keep quiet (ch. 24). Resulting sometimes in guilty acquiescence and sometimes in angry revolt, the disparity between what is publicly expected of her and her private sense of herself becomes the source of Lucy's feelings of unreality. Not the little girl lost (Polly), or the coquette (Ginevra), or the male manqué (Madame Beck), or the buried nun (in the garden), Lucy cannot be contained by the roles available to her. But neither is she free of them, since all these women do represent aspects of herself. Significantly, however, none of these roles ascribe to women the initiative, the intelligence, or the need to tell their own stories. Thus Lucy's evasions as a narrator indicate how far she (and all women) have come from silent submission and also how far all must yet go in finding a voice. In struggling against the confining forms she inherits, Lucy is truly involved in a mythic undertaking – an attempt to create an adequate fiction of her own. *Villette* is a novel that falls into two almost equally divided sections: the first part takes Lucy up to the episode of the confessional, and the second recounts her renewed attempt to make her own way in Madame Beck's establishment; but in the interlude at the Brettons' Brontë explores why and how the aesthetic conventions of patri- archal culture are as imprisoning for women as sexist economic, social and political institutions.

As in her other novels, Brontë charts a course of imprisonment, escape and exclusion until the heroine, near death from starvation, fortuitously discovers a family of her own. That Lucy has found some degree of self-knowledge through her illness is represented by her coincidental reunion with the Brettons. That she is in some ways healed is made apparent through her quarrel with Dr John Graham Bretton. Lucy refuses to submit to his view of Ginevra as a goddess, and after calling him a slave, she manages only to agree to differ with him. She sees him as a worshipper ready with the votive offering at the shrine of his favourite saint (ch. 18). In making this charge, she calls attention to the ways in which romantic love (like the spiritual love promulgated by the Catholic church) depends on coercion and slavery – on a loss of independence, freedom and self-respect for both the worshipper and the one worshipped.

Chapter 19, 'The Cleopatra', is crucial in elaborating this point. When Dr John takes Lucy sight-seeing to a museum, she is struck by the lounging self-importance of the painted heroine of stage and story. To slender Lucy, the huge Egyptian queen looks as absurdly inflated as the manner of her presentation: the enormous canvas is cordoned off, fronted by a cushioned bench for the adoring public. Lucy and her creator are plainly aware of the absurdity of such art, and Lucy has to struggle against the approbation which the monster painting seems to demand as its right. She refuses to treat the portrait as an autonomous entity, separate from reality, just as she defies the rhetoric of the religious paintings of 'La vie d'une femme' that M. Paul commends to her attention. The exemplary women in these portraits are 'Bloodless, brainless nonentities!' she exclaims, as vapid, interestingly, as 'ghosts', because they have nothing to do with life as Lucy knows it. Their piety and patience as young lady, wife, mother and widow leave her as cold as Cleopatra's voluptuous sensuality.

Of course the paintings are meant to examine the ridiculous roles men assign women, and thus the chapter is arranged to maximise the reader's consciousness of how varying male responses to female images are uniformly produced by the male pride that seeks to control women. In squeamish Dr John, who deposits and collects Lucy; voyeuristic M. Paul, who turns her away from Cleopatra while himself finding her 'Une femme superbe'; and foppish de Hamal, who minces daintily in front of the painting, Brontë describes the range of male responses to the completely sexual Cleopatra and the completely desexed, exemplary girl-wife-mother-widow, as Kate Millett has shown.[2]

In particular, because they parody Lucy's inner conflict between assertive sensuality and ascetic submission, the Cleopatra and 'La vie d'une femme' perpetuate the fallacy that one of these extremes can – or should – become an identity. Significantly, the rhetoric of the paintings and of the museum in which they are displayed is commercial, propagandistic and complacent: the paintings are valuable possessions, each with a message, each presented as a finished and admirable object. Just as commercial are the bourgeois arts at the concert Lucy attends with Dr John and his mother. Interestingly, it is here that Dr John decides that Ginevra Fanshawe is not even a pure-minded woman, much less a pure angel. But it is not simply his squeamishness about female sexuality that is illuminated on this occasion, for the very opulence of the concert hall testifies to the smugness of the arts practised there and the materialism of the people present.

Lucy's imagination, however, is touched by neither the paintings at the museum nor the performances at the civic concert because she resents the manipulation she associates with their magic. These arts are not ennobling because they seem egotistical, coercive, not unlike the grand processions 'of the church and the army – priests with relics, and soldiers with weapons' (ch. 36). In fact, declares Lucy, the Catholic church uses its theatrical ceremonies so that 'a Priesthood' – an apt emblem of patriarchy – 'might march straight on and straight upward to an all-dominating eminence' (ch. 36). Nevertheless, at the concert the illusions perpetrated by the architecture are successfully deceptive: everyone except Lucy seems unaware that the Queen is involved in a tragic drama with her husband, who is possessed by the same ghost that haunts Lucy, 'the spectre, Hypochondria' (ch. 20). The social and aesthetic conventions of the concert appear to cast a spell over the people, who are blinded to the King's actual state by the illusion of state pomp. The arts of the concert, like those of the museum and the church, perpetuate false myths that ensure the continuance of patriarchal forms, both secular and sacred, that are themselves devoid of intrinsic power or morality.

Although Dr John takes Lucy to see the actress Vashti only after she has left La Terrasse for the Rue Fossette, this dramatic performance is a fitting conclusion to Lucy's aesthetic excursions. Once again, the audience is the elite of Villette society. But this time Lucy's imagination is touched and she experiences the tremendous power of the artist: 'in the uttermost frenzy of energy is each maenad movement royally, imperially, incedingly upborne' (ch. 23). Certainly Lucy's description of Vashti is so fervently rhapsodic as to be almost incoherent. But most simply Vashti is a player of parts whose acting is destroying her. Therefore, as many critics have noted, 'this woman termed "plain"' (ch. 23) is a monitory image for Lucy, justifying her own reticence.[3] Indeed, at least one woman poet was drawn to Vashti because of this biblical queen's determination not to perform. The Black American poet Frances Harper wrote of a 'Vashti' who declares 'I never will be seen',[4] and Brontë's Vashti illuminates the impetus behind such a vow by demonstrating the annihilating power of the libidinal energies unleashed by artistic performance. Throughout the novel, Lucy has pleaded guiltless 'of that curse, an over-heated and discursive imagination' (ch. 2). But although she has tried to strike a bargain between the two sides of herself, buying an internal life of thought nourished by the 'necromantic joys' (ch. 8) of fancy at the high price of an external life limited to drudgery, the imaginative power cannot, Brontë shows, be contained in this way: it resurrects all those feelings that Lucy thought she had so ably put to death. During her mental breakdown, as we saw, her imagination recalled the dead in nightmares, roused the ghosts that haunted her, and transformed the dormitory into a replica of her own mind, a chamber of horrors.

Is the magic of art seen as necromantic for women because it revitalises females deadened by male myths? After she has returned to Madame Beck's, Lucy finds the release offered by the imagination quite tempting. Reason, the cruel teacher at the front of the room, is associated with frigid beds and barren board; but imagination is the winged angel that appeases with sweet foods and warmth. A daughter of heaven, imagination is the goddess from whom Lucy seeks solace:

> Temples have been reared to the Sun – altars dedicated to the Moon. Oh, greater glory! To thee neither hands build, nor lips consecrate: but hearts, through ages, are faithful to thy worship. *A dwelling thou hast, too wide for walls, too high for dome – a temple whose floors are space* – rites whose mysteries transpire in presence, to the kindling, the harmony of worlds!
>
> (ch. 21; italics ours)

Neither the male sun nor the female moon compare to this andro-gynous, imaginative power which cannot be contained or confined. But even as she praises the freedom, the expansiveness, of a force that transcends all limits, Lucy fears that, for her, the power-that-cannot-be-housed is never to be attained except in the dying dreams of an exile.

Beyond its representation of Lucy's subjective drama, the Vashti performance is also an important statement about the dangers of the imagination for all women. Vashti's passionate acting causes her to be rejected by proper society. Dr John, for instance, 'judged her as a woman, not an artist: it was a branding judgement' (ch. 23). But more profoundly important than his societal rejection is Vashti's own sense of being damned: 'Fallen, insurgent, banished, she remembers the heaven where she rebelled. Heaven's light, following her exile, pierces its confines, and discloses their forlorn remoteness' (ch. 23). Lucy had at first thought the presence on stage 'was only a woman'. But she 'found upon her something neither of woman nor of man: in each of her eyes sat a devil'. These evil forces wrote 'HELL' on her brow. They also 'cried sore and rent the tenement they haunted, but still refused to be exorcised'. The incarnation of 'Hate and Murder and Madness' (ch. 23), Vashti is the familiar figure we saw in *Frankenstein* and in *Wuthering Heights*, the Satanic Eve whose artistry of death is a testimonial to her fall from grace and her revolt against the tyranny of heaven as well as her revenge against the fall and the exile she re-enacts with each performance onstage.

Having experienced the origin of her own passions, Vashti will be punished for a rebellion that is decidedly futile for women. Certainly this is what Racine implies in *Phèdre*, which is the most famous and passionate role played by Vashti's historical prototype, the great French tragedienne Rachel.[5] But the violence of Vashti's acting – she stands onstage 'locked in struggle, rigid in resistance' – suggests that she is actually struggling against the fate of the character she plays, much as Lucy struggles against the uncongenial roles she plays. Vashti's resistance to 'the rape of every faculty' represents the plight of the female artist who tries to subvert the lessons of female submission implied – if not asserted – by art that damns the heroine's sexuality as the source of chaos and suffering. Because Vashti is portrayed as an uncontainable woman, her power will release a passion that engulfs not only the spectator but Vashti herself as well.

Twice Lucy interrupts her rhapsodic description of this actress to indicate that Vashti puts to shame the artist of the Cleopatra. Unlike the false artists who abound in *Villette*, Vashti uses her art not to manipulate others, but to represent herself. Her art, in other words, is confessional, unfinished – not a product, but an act; not an object meant to contain or coerce, but a personal utterance. Indeed, it is even a kind of strip show, a form of the female suicidal self-exposure that pornographers from Sade to the nameless producers of snuff films have exploited, so that her costly self-display recalls the pained ironic cry of Plath's 'Lady Lazarus': 'I turn and burn, / Do not think I underestimate your great concern.'[6] At the same time, Vashti's performance also inevitably reminds us of the dance of death the Queen must do in her fiery shoes at the end of 'Snow White'. But while Brontë presents Vashti's sufferings, she also emphasises that this art is a feminist reaction to patriarchal aesthetics, and so Lucy withholds the 'real' name of the actress and calls her, instead, 'Vashti'.

Unlike the queen of Villette, who seeks to solace her lord, or the queen of the Nile, who seems made for male pleasure, Queen Vashti of the Book of Esther refuses to placate King Ahasuerus. Quite gratuitously it seems, on the seventh day, when all patriarchs rest, the king calls on Vashti to display her beauty before the princes of the realm, and she refuses to come. Her revolt makes the princes fear that their wives will be filled with contempt for them. Brontë's actress, like the biblical queen, refuses to be treated as an object, and consciously rejects art that dehumanises its subject or its audience. By transcending the distinctions between private and public, between person and artist, between artist and art, Vashti calls into question, therefore, the closed forms of male culture. Like that of the biblical queen, her protest means the loss of her estate, banishment from the king's sight. And like sinister Lady Lazarus, who ominously warns that 'there is a charge, a very large charge, / For a word or a touch', Vashti puts on an inflammatory performance which so subverts the social order that it actually seems to set the theatre on fire and sends all the wealthy patrons rushing outside to save their lives. Even as her drama proposes an alternative to patriarchal culture, then, it defines the pain of female artistry, and the revengeful power of female rebellion.

*

Lucy, who has already employed image magic (in the burial of Dr John's letters), knows its powers are feeble compared to the fearsome but liberating force of the necromantic imagination (which dreams of their resurrection as golden hairs). Jane Eyre had experimented with these two very different arts in her dreamlike drawings (where we saw her unconscious impulses emerging prophetically) and in her portraits (where she didactically portrays beautiful Blanche Ingram in contrast to her own puny self to prove she has no chance with Rochester). More anxious than Jane about creativity, Lucy practises only the severely limited arts of sewing, tracing elaborate line engravings, and writing satiric sketches. Yet, by the time she describes the climactic park scenes, Lucy is an accomplished author. What has happened? To begin with, in the course of the novel she has learned to speak with her own voice, to emerge from the shadows: she defends her creed successfully against the persuasions of Père Silas and M. Paul; she speaks out for the lovers to Polly's father, and she stands up against Madame Beck's interference. All these advances are followed by moments of eclipse when she withdraws, but the sum progress is toward self-articulation, and self-dramatisation.

In the process of writing her story, moreover, Lucy has become less evasive. Her narrative increasingly defines her as the centre of her own concerns, the heroine of her own history. Her spirited capsule summaries of Polly's and Ginevra's romantic escapades prove that she sees the limits, even the comic aspects, of romantic love, and that another love, painful and constant and intellectual, is now more interesting to her. In fact, Lucy's plots have led not to burial but to exorcism, for she is in the process of becoming the author not only of her own life story but of her own life. It is for this reason that the subject of the ending of *Villette* is the problematic nature of the imagination. Having delineated the horrors of restraint and repression, Brontë turns to the possibility of a life consecrated to imagination, in part to come to terms with her own commitment to the creation of fictions that will no longer enslave women.

Bringing together all the characters and images in a grand finale, the park scenes are fittingly begun by the failure of Madame Beck's attempts to control Lucy. The administered sleeping potion does not drug but awakens her; escaping from the school that is now openly designated a den, a convent, and a dungeon, Lucy seems to have been roused by the necromantic imagination to sleepwalk through a dreamt, magical masque depicting her own quest for selfhood. Searching for the circular mirror, the stone basin of water in the moonlit, midnight summer park, Lucy discovers an enchanted place illuminated by the symbols of the imagination – a flaming arch of stars, coloured meteors, Egyptian architecture. Under a spell, in a magical, hallucinogenic world of apparitions and ghosts, she notes that 'on this whole scene was impressed a dream-like character: every shape was wavering, every movement floating, every voice echo-like – half-mocking, half-uncertain' (ch. 38). And the fact that this is a celebration commemorating a struggle for liberty does not destroy the marvel of such sights, because it so clearly reflects her own newly experienced freedom from constraint.[7] The allusions to art, the Eastern settings, the music, and the sense of magic remind us that Lucy's struggle is both psychological and aesthetic. So she refers to the park as a woody theatre, filled with actors engaged in discoveries that will lead to a climax (ch. 38) and a denouement (ch. 39).

In fact, the sequence of events in this dreamy midsummer *Walpurgisnacht* furnishes a microcosm of the novel, as Lucy's imagination summons up before her the spirits that have haunted her past and present life. First she sees the Brettons and commemorates her feeling for Graham in typically spatial terms, describing the tent of Peri Banou she keeps for him: folded in the hollow of her hand, it would expand into a tabernacle if released. Admitting for the first time her love for Dr John, she nevertheless avoids making herself known, moving on to watch the 'papist junta' composed of Père Silas, Madame Beck and Madame Walravens. As they wait for the arrival of Justine Marie, Lucy conjures up a vision of the dead nun. But she sees, instead, M. Paul arriving with his young ward, the niece named for the departed saint. Although she is jealous, Lucy feels that M. Paul's nun has now finally been buried, and at this point of great suffering, she begins to praise the goddess of truth. As she has repeatedly, Lucy is advocating repression, although it requires her to re-enact the conflict between Jael and Sisera, the pain of self-crucifixion. When 'the iron [has] entered well [her] soul', she finally believes she has been 'renovated'.

Significantly, on her return to the school Lucy finds what seems to be the nun of the garret sleeping in her bed. Now, however, she can at last defy the spectre, for the park scene appears to have liberated her, enabling her to destroy this symbol of her chastity and confinement. Why does the appearance of Paul's nun lead to the surfacing of Lucy's? As always, Brontë uses the plot to suggest an answer. Following her imagination on the night of the park festival, Lucy had escaped the convent and, in doing so, she had left the door ajar, thus effecting the escape of Ginevra and de Hamal – the dandy who we now learn has been using the nun's disguise to court the coquette. We have already seen how Ginevra and de Hamal represent the self-gratifying, sensual, romantic side of Lucy. Posturing before mirrors, the fop and the coquette are vacuous but for the roles they play. Existing only in the 'outside' world, they have no more sense of self than the nun whose life is completely 'internal'. Thus, for Lucy to liberate herself from Ginevra and de Hamal means that she can simultaneously rid herself of the self-denying nun. In fact, these mutually dependent spirits have been cast out of her house because, in the park, unable to withdraw into voyeurism, she experienced jealousy. Hurt without being destroyed, she has at least temporarily liberated herself from the dialectic of her internal schism. And to indicate once again how that split is a male fiction, Brontë shows us how the apparently female image of the nun masks the romantic male plots of de Hamal.

What is most ironic about this entire sequence, however, is that Lucy is wrong: Paul is committed to her, not to the memory of the buried Justine Marie, or to his ward. But, because she is wrong, she is saved. Imagination has led her astray throughout the park scene – conjuring up an image of a calm and shadowy park and then leading her to believe that she can exist invisibly in the illuminated festival, causing her to picture Madame Beck in her bed and M. Paul on shipboard, creating the romantic story of Paul and his rich, beautiful ward. It is with relieved self-mockery that Lucy laughs at her own panegyric to the so-called goddess of truth, whose message is really only an imaginative projection of her own worst fears. Ultimately, indeed, the entire distinction between imagination and reason breaks down in the park scenes because Lucy realises that what she has called 'Reason' is really repressive witchcraft or image magic that would transform her into a nun. Although Lucy leaves the park thinking that the calm, white, stainless moon triumphs – a witness of 'truth all regnant' (ch. 39) – the next day she cannot accept the truth. And though she views it as a weakness, this very inability to acquiesce in silence is a sign of her freedom from the old internal struggle, for Lucy has emerged from the park a more integrated person, able to express herself in the most threatening circumstances. Now she can even defy Madame Beck to catch at a last chance to speak with Paul, detaining him with her cry: 'My heart will break!' (ch. 41).

And, albeit with terrible self-consciousness, Lucy can now ask Paul whether her appearance displeases him. This question climaxes a series of scenes before the mirror, each of which defines Lucy's sense of herself. When, at the beginning of the book, Ginevra shows Lucy an image of herself with no attractive accomplishments, no beauty, no chance of love, the girl accepts the reflection with satiric calm, commending Ginevra's honesty. Midway through the novel, however, at the concert, she experiences a 'jar of discord, a pang of regret' (ch. 20) at the contrast between herself in a pink dress and the handsome Brettons. Finally, when she thinks she has lost the last opportunity of seeing Paul, she feelingly perceives herself alone – sodden, white, with swollen and glassy eyes (ch. 38). Instead of seeing the mirror-image as the object of another person's observations, Lucy looks at herself by herself. Increasingly able to identify herself with her body, she is freed from the contradictory and stultifying definitions of her provided by all those who think they know her, and she begins to understand how Dr John, Mr Home,

Ginevra, and even Polly see her in a biased way. At last, Brontë suggests, Lucy has learned that imaginative 'projection' and reasoned 'apprehension' of the 'truth' are inseparable. The mirror does not reflect reality; it creates it by interpreting it. But the act of interpretation can avoid tyranny when it remains just that – a perceptual act. After all, 'wherever an accumulation of small defences is found . . . there, be sure, it is needed' (ch. 27).

It is this mature recognition of the necessity and inadequacy of self-definition – this understanding of the need for fictions that assert their own limits by proclaiming their personal usefulness – that wins for Lucy finally a room of her own, indeed, a house of her own. The school in the Faubourg Clotilde is a fitting conclusion to her struggle and to the struggles of all of Brontë's heroines for a comfortable space. The small house has large, vine-covered windows. The salon is tiny, but pretty, with delicate walls tinged like a blush and a brilliant carpet covering the highly waxed floor. The small furniture, the plants, the diminutive kitchenware please Lucy. Not by any means a dwelling too wide for walls or too high for dome, her tidy house represents on the one hand the lowering of her sights and on the other her willingness to begin making her own way, even if on a small scale.

Both a home and a school, the house represents Lucy's independence: upstairs are two sleeping-rooms and a schoolroom – no attic mentioned. Here, on the balcony overlooking the gardens of the faubourg, near a water-jet rising from a nearby well, Paul and Lucy commemorate their love in a simple meal that consists of chocolate, rolls, and fresh red fruit. Although he is her king, her provider only rents the house himself and she will quickly have to earn her keep: Lucy has escaped both the ancestral mansion and the convent. And so, under the moonlight that is now an emblem of her imaginative power to define her own truths, she is more fortunate than Shirley because she actually experiences the days of 'our great Sire and Mother'; she can 'taste that grand morning's dew – bathe in its sunrise' (ch. 41).

Unlike Caroline Helstone, moreover, Lucy is given real food, for she is to be sustained by Paul, even in his absence: 'he would give neither a stone, nor an excuse – neither a scorpion, nor a disappointment; his letters were real food that nourished, living water that refreshed' (ch. 42). Nevertheless, despite her hope that women can obtain a full, integrated sense of themselves *and* economic independence *and* male affection, Brontë also recognises that such a wish must not be presented falsely as an accomplished fact. The ambiguous ending of *Villette* reflects Lucy's ambivalence, her love for Paul and her recognition that it is only in his absence that she can exert herself fully to exercise her own powers. It also reflects Brontë's determination to avoid the tyrannical fictions that have traditionally victimised women. Once more, she deflates male romanticism. Although her lover sails off on the *Paul et Virginie*, although her novel – like Bernadin de Saint Pierre's – ends in shipwreck, Brontë insists again that it is the confined woman, Lucy, who waits at home for the adventuring male, but notes that the end of love must not be equated with the end of life. The last chapter of *Villette* begins by reminding us that 'Fear sometimes imagines a vain thing' (ch. 42). It ends with Lucy's refusal to end conclusively: 'Leave sunny imaginations hope' (ch. 42). Brontë gives us an open-ended, elusive fiction, refraining from any definitive message except to remind us of the continued need for sustaining stories of survival.

The very erratic way Lucy tells the story of becoming the author of her own life illustrates how Brontë produces not a literary object but a literature of consciousness. Just as Brontë has become Lucy Snowe for the writing of *Villette*, just as Lucy has become all her characters, we submit to the spell of the novel, to the sepulchral voice relating truths of the dead revivified by the necromancy of the imagination. Brontë rejects not only the confining images conferred on women by patriarchal art, but the implicitly coercive nature of that art. *Villette* is not meticulously crafted. The very excess of its style, as well as the ambiguous relationship between its author and its heroine, declare Brontë's commitment to the personal processes of writing and reading. In place of the ecstatic or philosophic egotistical sublime, she offers us something closer to the qualified experience of what Keats called 'negative capability'. Making her fiction a parodic, confessional utterance that can only be understood through the temporal sequences of its plot, Brontë criticises the artists she considers in *Villette* – Rubens, Schiller, Bernadin de Saint Pierre, Wordsworth, Arnold, and others.

It is ironic that her protest could not save her from being the subject of one of Arnold's poetic complaints on the early death of poets. In 'Haworth Churchyard' Arnold recognises how Brontë's art is lit by intentionality when he describes how she told 'With a Master's accent her feign'd History of passionate life'. But his insistence on desexing her art – here, by describing her 'Master's accent', later by referring to her with a masculine pronoun[8] – shows him to be the first of a long line of readers who could not or would not submit to a reading process and a realisation so totally at odds with his own life, his own art and criticism.

It is the act of receptivity that Brontë uses to subvert patriarchal art. Recently some feminists have been disturbed that Brontë did not reject the passivity of her heroines.[9] As we have seen, her books do elaborate on the evils of equating masculinity with power and femininity with submission. But Brontë knew that the habit of submission had bequeathed a vital insight to women – a sympathetic imagination that could help them, in their revolt, from becoming like their masters. Having been obliged to experience themselves as objects, women understand both their need and their capacity for awakening from a living death; they know it is necromancy, not image magic – a resurrecting confessional art, not a crucifying confessional penance – which can do this without entangling yet another Other in what they have escaped. Conscious of the politics of poetics, Brontë is, in some ways, a phenomenologist – attacking the discrepancy between reason and imagination, insisting on the subjectivity of the objective work of art, choosing as the subject of her fiction the victims of objectification, inviting her readers to experience with her the interiority of the Other. For all these reasons she is a powerful precursor for all the women who have been strengthened by the haunted and haunting honesty of her art.

From Sandra M. Gilbert and Susan Gubar, *The Madwoman in the Attic: The Woman Writer and the Nineteenth-Century Literary Imagination* (New Haven, 1979), pp. 416–25, 433–40.

NOTES

[The scope and ambition of Gilbert and Gubar's massive study from which this excerpt is taken is indicated by the subtitle. Gilbert and Gubar seek to identify the common features of women's writing in the nineteenth century and hence by implication its difference from men's writing. In its endeavour to outline a 'feminist poetics' *The Madwoman* represented a significant advance in theoretical sophistication for feminist literary criticism. Gilbert and Gubar argue that the absence of literary 'mothers' for women writers in the nineteenth century exposes the inadequacy of Harold Bloom's 'anxiety of influence' as a theory of women's literary creativity. They conclude that in a culture that defined creativity as masculine, women writers suffered instead from a debilitating 'anxiety of authorship'. According to their central thesis, in the face of this anxiety women writers 'managed the difficult task of achieving true female literary authority by simultaneously conforming to and subverting patriarchal literary standards' (p. 73). *The Madwoman* has subsequently been criticised for the totalising aspect of both its representation of patriarchal ideology as monolithically oppressive and its reading of women's writing as inevitably 'revisionary and revolutionary'. However, in brilliantly highlighting the importance of subversive subtexts in women's writing, Gilbert and Gubar were instrumental in opening up one of the most fruitful areas of feminist literary enquiry. All quotations in this excerpt are from *Villette* (New York: Harper Colophon, 1972). Ed.]

1. E. M. Forster, *Aspects of the Novel* (New York, 1964), pp. 92–3.

2. Kate Millett, *Sexual Politics* (New York, 1971), p. 198. [See p. 36 above.]

3. Robert Martin, *The Accents of Persuasion: Charlotte Brontë's Novels* (New York, 1966), pp. 160–6. See Andrew D. Hook, 'Charlotte Brontë, the Imagination, and *Villette*', in *The Brontës: A Collection of Critical Essays*, ed. Ian Gregor (Englewood Cliffs, NJ, 1970), for an excellent discussion of Lucy's incoherence in describing Vashti, p. 151. Vashti's story appears in the Book of Esther, 1:1 to 2:18.

4. Frances Harper, 'Vashti', in *Early Black American Poets*, ed. William Robinson (Iowa, 1969), pp. 34–6.

5. In *Charlotte Brontë* (Oxford, 1967), p. 481, Winifred Gérin explains that Rachel was most famous for her passionate role in *Phèdre*, but that Charlotte Brontë saw her act the 'milder' roles of Camille in Corneille's *Les Trois Horaces* and Adrienne in *Adrienne Lecouvreur*.

6. Sylvia Plath, 'Lady Lazarus', *Ariel* (New York, 1966), pp. 6–9.

7. Earl A. Knies, *The Art of Charlotte Brontë* (Ohio, 1969), p. 194.

8. Matthew Arnold's 'Haworth Churchyard' originally appeared in *Fraser's Magazine*, May 1855, and is reprinted in *The Brontës: The Critical Heritage*, ed. Miriam Allott (London, 1974), pp. 306–10.

9. Patricia Beer, '*Reader, I Married Him*' (London, 1974), pp. 84–126, and Patricia Meyer Spacks, *The Female Imagination* (New York, 1975), pp. 70–2.

4

Substance and Shadow: Reading Reality in 'Villette'

TONY TANNER

Since there is so much available material considering *Villette* as a
Victorian novel and relating it to Charlotte Brontë's life and her
other novels, I want to consider the novel from a more general
perspective – as a study in how a human being attempts to constitute
herself in a society largely indifferent to her needs. In this connection
I wish to invoke some terms of Sartre's before considering in some
detail the structuring of the novel. Sartre, on different occasions, has
defined the origin of action in the structure of the human being as
'*lack*, as ontological privation, attempting to satisfy itself, to fulfill
itself, and thereby to arrive at some definitive state of being': he has
also described it as '*need*', which is little more than a translation of
the ontological terminology into a relatively more socio-economic
kind. 'Just as lack, as an abstract way of characterizing human
existence, takes place in a world abstractly characterized as *contingent*, whose essential structure, with respect to man, is *facticity* (that
is to say, incommensurability with human thought and human
existence) ... so in these new concrete terms, in which man's
emptiness takes the form of *need*, the resistance of the world to man
is now defined in terms of *scarcity*. For scarcity is precisely the
unanalysable starting point, the contingent datum, of the world in
which we exist. Unintelligible in itself, simply a fact to which we
cannot assign any metaphysical significance whatsoever, it nonetheless is the framework in which we must act, and conditions and
alienates our acts and projects even in their very conception.' (The

quotations are from Frederic Jameson in *Marxism and Form*[1].) This borrowing of modern European terminology to initiate a consideration of the plight of a Victorian heroine is not part of an attempt to turn her into a contemporary outsider. It is rather to introduce the suggestion that some of the problems considered by writers like Sartre in attempts to define man's position in the given world are latent in a visible if inchoate form in this remarkable novel. It pursues some of the problems posed by Victorian society for the unlocated individual to an extreme point, a point at which they begin to be recognisable as early forms of problems which served increasingly to characterise that society as it developed into the one we know now. Lucy Snowe's apparently rather contained domestic drama is a drama based very much on lack and need, and the experience of 'facticity' (simply meaning things incommensurable with her own thoughts) and scarcity, and the problems involved in forming 'projects' is one to which she herself refers. Looking carefully into the conditions of her life we can begin to see outlines and arrangements which can enable us to return to our own condition with a heightened awareness.

*

In this problematic world of substance and shadow, it is surprising how few direct physical contacts there are, apart from such minor intrusions as Ginevra's insistence on taking Lucy's arm or leaning on her. In the prowling, peeping world of confining and darkened rooms which centres in Madame Beck's, physicality is for the most part sedulously avoided. (Note that even Paul is a spy with a special concealed 'post of observation' in a lattice. Lucy's comment on this habit of secret observation is remarkable. ' "Monsieur, I tell you every glance you cast from the lattice is a wrong done to the best part of your own nature. To study the human heart thus is to banquet in secret and sacrilegiously on Eve's apples." ' In one sentence Charlotte Brontë points to a problem which was to obsess later novelists like Hawthorne and James – the moral ambiguity of the position of the 'observer'. From one point of view to take up a disinterested position *vis-à-vis* society and treat it as a spectacle is the obvious way for an artist, particularly one to any degree alienated from that society, to gain the perceptual material for his study of its inhabitants. But at the same time there grew up the feeling that it was somehow a violation of the sacred otherness of people to treat them as objects of analytic scrutiny without venturing the risk of direct contact and relational participation.) In the devious world of *Villette*, mainly in the foreign

territories of Brussels, everyone spies on everyone else, the watcher is
watched with a minimum of eye-to-eye contact, though there is quite
a lot of indirect watching, for instance by the use of mirrors (even
Lucy is perforce an observer). It is a very voyeuristic world. The two
main physical acts of direct contact in the book are Paul's blow to the
face of Madame Beck, and his kissing Lucy, but it is notable that
these two most intimate acts of aggression and love are not really
seen, indeed hardly described – we infer them from gaps in the text
which seem to indicate a deliberate refusal to name such non-verbal
actions.

But if the body as such is almost denied as an active presence
(people being for the most part described by what they wear, or their
faces registered in physiognomic terms) then 'affect' is transferred to
its secondary manifestations. (It might be objected that Graham is
presented directly as a physically handsome man, an erotic figure,
but Lucy admires him from afar and he is experienced more as a
romantic stereotype, a copy of a copy, but not a sexual presence. He
is a dream figure projected out of deprivation and solitude. The man
who is most intensely registered physically is Paul Emanuel although
his erotic power is hardly admitted until the end.) A good example of
these secondary manifestations is the attention paid to the particular
quality of noise of a person's tread. Thus when Lucy is lost and
helpless in Villette and she is helped by a kind stranger (Graham as it
turns out) she follows him as he guides her through the city with
almost devotional gratitude: 'I believe I would have followed that
frank tread, through continual night, to the world's end.' And near
the conclusion when she is waiting without hope to see Paul Emanuel
before he sails, her attention is aroused by a step: 'I vaguely and
momentarily wondered to hear the step of but one "ouvrier". I
noted, too – as captives in dungeons find sometimes dreary leisure to
note the merest trifles – that this man wore shoes, and not sabots: I
concluded that it must be the master-carpenter, coming to inspect
before he sent his journeymen. I threw round me my scarf. He
advanced; he opened the door; my back was towards it; I felt a little
thrill – a curious sensation, too quick and transient to be analysed.'
This is a good example of how Charlotte Brontë introduces suspense
and nervous excitement into her account: the advance of the
unnamed figure, the change of tempo from dreariness to 'thrill', the
sentence made up of short phrases separated by semi-colons working
like a series of accelerating palpitations. But what starts it all is the
obviously habitual deciphering of a step or tread. When the direct

confrontation of faces tends to be avoided then the sound of feet becomes of heightened significance. This is not fetishism exactly, though it could certainly lead to that, but more part of that avoidance or denial of the body which I think is one result of inhabiting this curiously confused world of substance and shadow.

In considering the various problems surrounding the idea of 'materiality' in this book one more word should be noted – 'magic'. Lucy's sense of being in a world suddenly transformed by magic occurs most notably on two occasions; both take place when she is away from Madame Beck's and seems to enter an estranged and enchanted world, one in which the very ontological status of the external solid world becomes entirely problematical, partly due to her own heightened and disordered consciousness. The first occasion is the visit to Madame Walravens (ch. 34) in which, as she tries to make out a picture, 'it rolled back into nothing', then the wall falls away to 'let in phantoms'. When Madame Walravens looms up as some kind of shapeless malign presence, Lucy's problem is 'was it actual substance?' and all that happens and the strange surroundings seem to be 'parts of a fairy tale'. This is of course in the Gothic tradition, but the experience is not offered for any kind of narrative *frisson* but rather to project the kind of epistemological unease which can beset Lucy in her displaced condition. Similarly on the famous night walk through the city on the occasion of the town festival when Lucy, under the influence of opium, wanders through the streets in a state of intense excitement, everything loses its familiarity and becomes 'a land of enchantment'. Robert Heilman in his famous essay on Charlotte Brontë's ' "New" Gothic' says of this scene: 'This is a surrealistic, trance-like episode which makes available to fiction a vast new territory and idiom.'[2] This is to say, Charlotte Brontë is exploring states of mind on the extreme edge of mental disorder, and following out ranges of sensation and response, new 'readings' of reality, which slip away from the constraining bourgeois house of consciousness ('eat your supper, drink your wine, oubliez les anges, les bossues, et surtout, les professeurs'), just as Lucy slips away from Madame Beck's house in the night as all the doors seem 'almost spontaneously to unclose without the creak of a hinge or click of a latch'. These are the very doors of the domesticated consciousness, and following her resolve to let 'Imagination' dominate over 'Matter' Lucy does indeed become 'alive to new thought'. She enters a world of new colours, sounds, music, and lights – we would now probably speak of 'expanded consciousness' – and encounters the 'strangest architectural wealth – of altar and of temple, of pyramid, obelisk and sphinx; incredible to say, the wonders and the symbols of Egypt teemed throughout the park of Villette'. No matter that this strange architectural intrusion is explicable as being part of the pasteboard decorations for the festival. Lucy's excursion into a dream-like world, hallucinatory and apparitional, is an authentic psychological excursus beyond the bounds of normal modes of perception via a feverish illness which leads her to experience a world metamorphosed and transformed. Significantly she enters the park where the festival is being held, not through the gate, which is locked and guarded by soldiers, but through a gap in the paling which she had unconsciously noticed without realising she remembered it. This is a perfect projection in topographical terms of an area of consciousness bypassing the militant guardianship of the censor through a 'gap' in the defences which had entered on an unconscious level as a memory trace and only now comes to the surface of the mind in its fevered state. The instinctive object of her quest is, note, the stone basin in the park 'brimming with cool water'. References to cups, bowls, basins, etc., empty or full, abound in the metaphoric dimension of the text. It is unnecessary to proliferate examples or spell out possible implications. Her very use of the metaphor of some longed-for water to fill up an emptiness relates to her experience of 'lack', and her longing to find a connection with some flowing energy and life which has been eliminated by the aridities and rigidities of the surface of contemporary life. (It is not uncommon as a metaphor in Victorian literature.) In addition, her quest may also indicate an inclination to tap hidden reserves in the well of her own unconscious. In terms of the book this is no accidentally induced drug trip. For Lucy, who often thinks in geographic and literary-mythic terms, the 'wonders and symbols of Egypt' *do* 'teem through the park of Villette', in the sense that there is a part of her mind where exotic phenomena and non-Christian symbols flow on, even while the rest of her mind is narrowed down to negotiate the hard day-time realities of Villette. In this incident the separation is temporarily dissolved, and the realities of the unconscious assert themselves. What the episode tells her, in unspoken language, is that in the midst of matter we are in magic. The tyranny of the 'substantial' is temporarily dispelled as consciousness roams beyond customary bounds into, indeed, a kind of 'chaos', and finds non-habitual resources within itself. That this is an aberrational way of perceiving is underlined by the presence at the festival of most of the other main characters in the book behaving quite normally to each other. And Lucy is far from achieving 'true vision' as she makes all kinds of incorrect inferences from what she sees, detecting cabals where there are only contingencies. Yet there is a kind of rightness in her deranged vision, for she does indeed live in a plotting world, and if it is an aberrational mode of perception it is one which Lucy has been approaching in her consistent refusal to regard her environment in preordained ways. It is her most extreme step (albeit partly involuntary) beyond the frame which society places round cognition, dictating that reality can only be seen in a certain way. This venture beyond the conventional cognitive frame is both exciting and painful, and it is brief. It is, in Beckett's words, one of those 'perilous zones in the life of the individual . . . when for a moment the boredom of living is replaced by the suffering of being'.

*

A first person narrative using a narrator not identical with the author offers a text with three different levels of language. There is the invisible presence of Charlotte Brontë; there is the narrator Lucy Snowe who is turning her experiences into a linguistic arrangement or discourse; and there is the Lucy Snowe whose utterance and actions are contained within the events being narrated, or the story. These last two could be considered by using the terms of the Russian Formalists who distinguished between tale – the sequence of events represented, as they would happen in life – and plot – the particular arrangement and presentation of these events by the narrator. The point of making these perhaps rather obvious distinctions is to remind ourselves that we should not only look *through* the text at the events – the struggles of a poor governess abroad and how she finally won the love of one of the teachers, etc. We must also look *at* the text, not as a separate act of stylistic analysis to offer a contribution to a study of narrative language in the mid-nineteenth century, but as being the creative event or action which concerns us most as readers. What Lucy Snowe makes of her life as narrative is as important as what she experienced prior to writing it. It is indeed an extension of life as well as a reconstruction of it, the important difference being that as experiencing subject she had little control over her environment but as narrating subject she has complete linguistic control over its representation. The words are of course all Charlotte Brontë's, but we must see the narrative arrangement as Lucy Snowe's. For it is in the 'how' of her describing – other people, her own sufferings and tensions, the oscillations of her life – that she most effectively asserts her identity and her freedom. The amplitude, and wholeness, found in the telling contain and compensate for the privation and sickness experienced in the living. (What is particularly distinctive about the mode of telling, or 'style' in Charlotte Brontë has been very ably and completely analysed by Margot Peters[3].)

As Margot Peters points out there is an unusual amount of violence in the metaphoric language of the book, a violence which accords not with the exernal events which, as I have tried to show, oscillate between an absence of action which may be experienced as boredom or tranquillity, and sudden interruptions of routine, whether it be a strange object or apparition disturbing her retreat and reverie in the school garden, or Paul Emanuel erupting into the schoolroom. The violence is experienced internally, on the nerves, in the pulse rate, in the mind, and this violence is projected in the non-social areas of her prose, for internality finds its most ample space for expression in the realm of metaphor. Thus, to give just one example, while in her external actions she may not do anything much more violent than breaking the points off her scissors, in her inner world she can write of invoking 'Conviction' to 'nail' her 'with the strongest spikes her strongest strokes could drive'. The metaphoric realm, extended in many directions through geographic comparisons, endless literary and Biblical allusions, and a personal vocabulary ranging from extremes of masochism to all kinds of fervencies of anxiety, anticipation, and passion, has an unquestioned authority and a privileged status which it does not enjoy, for example, in Jane Austen's prose, where a corrected social language is ultimately allowed to dominate. The reason for this is clear and points not only to the difference between the two novelists but to one of the central facts about Charlotte Brontë's work. For Jane Austen, the social world was the ultimate realm of reality, no matter what internal miseries and struggles and isolations may be experienced within it. For Charlotte Brontë this social reality with its authoritative norms and finally acceptable values had gone, and metaphors take the place of this lost society. Particularly for Lucy Snowe in her displaced situation in Madame Beck's 'hollow system', where all is stealth, uncertainty, and latent hostility, there are not only no ordained values structured into the environment, there are not even any epistemological certainties. She has to grope her way through a world in which both morality and reality have been rendered totally dubious, amorphous, at times unreal. Her two most extreme experiences – alone in an empty school in a foreign land with only a cretin for company, and alone in the town on the night of the festival when everything appears deformed to her unregulated senses – point to that mixture of defamiliarised void and decontextualised vividness which in more muted forms is her daily experience. There are objects and there are people and places, but what they mean, how they cohere, and above all what her place among them all is and how she is to relate to them – these are questions she is constantly having to ask and, with no real help from the environment, she is constantly having to project private and provisional answers. In a word, she finds herself in 'bad' narrative in which she has effectively to create, or put together, her own ontology and value-system. Europe and even parts of England are geographical equivalents of an estranged world in which there is no transactional trust (except for the brief moment she achieves with Paul Emanuel, which is almost immediately obliterated) and no secular reassurances. If she thinks monadically instead of socially that is because that is the situation which, as an isolated female outsider, she finds herself in. The company which is most real to her is, for the most part, the many biblical and literary references which she has internalised. But these are books from vanished ages, so there is a constant tension for her between an alien present world and familiar absent texts. Lacking any proper social context she has, as it were, to find a context for herself from within, using the imaginative, moral and religious literature which form her most valuable 'luggage'.

Hence the overwhelming importance of her own narrative. It is not a matter of fond recall, or even of the consolations of recollection. It is in part an act of retrospective exegesis but more than that it is the creation of a narrative context of private semantic amplitude and significance to set against the social context of constricted and insufficient meaning which she had to endure. At one point in that experience Père Silas tries to convert her to Catholicism and she writes, 'I might just now, instead of writing this heretic narrative, be counting my beads in the cell of a certain Carmelite convent.' This offers a paradigm of the extremes open to her. Either to accept a form of 'imprisonment' in foreign society, numbing her consciousness with the endless repetition of the formulations of an alien creed; or to create her own narrative space in which she can allow her consciousness to expand, and where she can reinvent the world of her experience in and on her own terms. In the largest sense of the word, it is in her 'heretic' narrative that she can find the freedom to define herself as an individual, and as a woman. Thus although *Villette* follows aspects of Charlotte Brontë's life more closely than any of her other novels, it is not to be seen as veiled autobiography. Nor is it just a picture of herself 'seen heroically or despairingly' in Gertrude Stein's terms. Just as Charlotte Brontë hands over to Lucy Snowe the right to rename her actual environment (Villette, Labassecour, Boue-Marine, etc.) so her whole book is an act of renomination. As she composes her book she is composing herself, and what that book shows us is not just Charlotte Brontë in a refracted light but the imagined figure of Lucy Snowe refusing to have her experience named for her. For just as society seeks to impose roles on her, so it would 'write' her existence for her if she let it. Lucy Snowe, depicting herself in various stages of ignorance, illness, and incompletion finally defines herself in her 'heretic narrative'. The meaning of the life only finds itself in the completing of the book. That book ambiguously entitled *Villette* is, then, not only a fictional account of a young Victorian woman seeking to establish herself in midnineteenth-century Brussels; it is also a dramatisation of her mapping out the 'small town' of her existence. This is the completion of her final 'project', the fulfilment of that 'lack' and 'need' which marked her original condition, and thus her arrival 'at some definitive state of being'.

From *Villette*, ed. Tony Tanner (Penguin, 1979), pp. 10–11, 24–9, 47–51.

NOTES

[This extract, taken from Tony Tanner's Introduction to the Penguin edition of *Villette*, is the first of three essays in this volume which focus very specifically on the narrative act in Brontë's novel. In his Introduction Tanner is centrally concerned with 'the self without society' and the ways in which problems of interrelation manifest themselves as problems of communication. His interest in the narrative act stems not so much from a preoccupation with stylistics as from a recognition of the potential for oppression or liberation in language itself. In Tanner's terms, individuals can be regarded as being 'beyond the reach or comprehension of society simply by an inadequacy and narrowness of terminology' (p. 39). Hence, the crucial nature of the endeavour to extend the 'language of illness' (p. 39). Tanner's Introduction also provides a fascinating discussion of 'materiality' in the novel, drawing parallels between the topography of Lucy's inner and outer world, and considering the ways in which characters are regarded as 'objects of analytic scrutiny' rather than encountered relationally in their 'otherness'. Ed.]

1. Frederick Jameson, *Marxism and Form* (Princeton, 1971). [Ed.]

2. Robert Heilman, 'Charlotte Brontë's "New" Gothic', in *The Victorian Novel: Modern Essays in Criticism*, ed. Ian Watt (New York, 1971). [Ed.]

3. Margot Peters, *Charlotte Brontë: Style in the Novel* (Madison, 1973), [Ed.]

5

'Faithful Narrator' or 'Partial Eulogist': First-Person Narration in Brontë's 'Villette'

NANCY SORKIN RABINOWITZ

Charlotte Brontë's *Villette* is a striking text in at least three often commented upon ways: the first-person narrator does not tell us all she knows, the text is open, and the 'hero' is sacrificed to enable the growth of the heroine. But these tend to be seen as isolated features of the text. Thus, recent criticism of the text seems to have focused either on the narrative strategies employed,[1] or on the plot, questioning the extent of Lucy Snowe's freedom from social constraints, particularly the compulsion to (heterosexual) love and marriage.[2] As I hope to show, the two formal elements are not only connected, but they are used to forward Brontë's attempt to mark out new paths for women. In *Villette*, Brontë develops both a poetics and politics of denial, a means for the oppressed to empower themselves.

We can better see the connections between the three aspects if we compare *Villette* to the earlier *Jane Eyre*. Given the success of that novel, it is interesting that Brontë departs from the model it provides as she tells the story of another teacher similar to Jane in many respects.[3] While Jane is a trustworthy narrator of her own life, at crucial points Lucy deceives us. This change in strategy is correlated to the other formal change (*Villette*'s ending is open where *Jane Eyre*'s is closed) and to changes in the plot, where we are accustomed

68

to looking for ideology (Lucy is [although only presumably] alone and with a career, while Jane Eyre is married). In both the aesthetic and the ethical domains, then, *Villette* is a far more radical novel than the earlier *Jane Eyre*.[4]

I would like to take up the challenge of Mary Jacobus, who calls our task in speaking of *Villette* 'not to explain away, but to explain – to theorize – the incoherencies and compromises, inconsistencies and dislocations ...'.[5] We are helped in this endeavour by recent essays in feminist criticism which have focused attention on ways in which female texts alter male forms in order to avoid male constructions of female experience. Nancy Miller, working on the perception of women's texts as unrealistic or lacking in verisimilitude, has conceptualised the problem in the following way:

> The blind spot here is both political (or philosophical) and literary. It does not see, nor does it want to, that the fictions of desire behind the desiderata of fiction are masculine and not universal constructs. It does not see that the maxims that pass for the truth of human experience, and the encoding of that experience in literature, are organisations, when they are not fantasies, of the dominant culture. To read women's literature is to see and hear repeatedly a chafing against the 'unsatisfactory reality' contained in the maxim.[6]

Working from Miller's insight, I would suggest that Brontë is using Lucy Snowe's deceptions to escape the dictated conventions of the realistic form. Author and narrator reject the maxims of behaviour available to them and develop a sense of female power, to be gained in part through the act of narration.[7] The maxims are overt in the text; Lucy depends on 'maxims of philosophy' to console Polly (ch. III), and M. Paul speaks in maxims about women and bids her study 'La vie d'une femme' (ch. XIX). Such maxims are not merely self-referential, about the possibilities available to women in literature, but also refer to the world, and the possibilities available there. Sandra Gilbert and Susan Gubar, in considering the duplicity of the narrator, connect life and literary work, commenting that:

> Obviously, Lucy's life, her sense of herself, does not conform to the literary or social stereotypes provided by her culture to define and circumscribe female life. ... So she finds herself using and abusing – presenting and undercutting – images and stories of male devising, even as she omits or elides what has been deemed unsuitable, improper or aberrant in her own experience.[8]

Brontë allows Lucy to come to develop her own mode of discourse, but she does not stop there. In turning away from the division of labour that gives men the world and women love,[9] Brontë gives Lucy meaningful work as well.

I

What does Lucy do that leads Robert Martin to call her unreliable and Gilbert and Gubar to call her a voyeur? She is not an obviously unreliable narrator, like that of *Notes from the Underground* or Jason in *The Sound and the Fury*, where the reader must distance her/himself from the narrator's judgements. In general, Lucy's character judgements are very good – about Ginevra, Mme Beck, and even John Graham Bretton. But on one or two occasions, Lucy Snowe actually withholds information with the intention of misleading us, for instance, as to when she recognises Bretton.[10] She does this even though she explicitly raises the issue of truth and falsity and presumably accepts her obligation to be a 'faithful narrator and not partial eulogist' to Dr John (ch. XIX). It is not that she tries to deceive us entirely, since she tells us later and draws attention to her own behaviour. Therefore, there must be another purpose for this strategy. Looking at the most egregious examples of duplicity, perhaps we can see what Brontë/Lucy gain by this calculated dishonesty.

Lucy's most commented upon and most clearly gratuitous falsehood is in her failure to tell the reader that she has recognised that Dr John is the Graham she had known ten years before. There are several levels in the process, and Dr John never does find out all that Lucy knows. First, Dr John is the same man who met Lucy at the station when she first arrived in Villette. We are told this immediately, so that Lucy and we share this information throughout, but she never tells Dr John. On this occasion, Lucy does not justify herself, but we can hypothesise that her reticence allows her to keep that memory intact. Similarly, she later keeps the letters she receives from Dr John even though their ownership is problematic: Dr John calls the lost one 'his' letter and threatens to keep it from 'the grovelling, groping monomaniac' Lucy (ch. XXII). By not telling him of the original encounter, she remains the sole owner of the incident and therefore does not undergo the risk of that diminution.

Second, Lucy recognises Dr John as Graham in chapter X, but she does not tell him or us until chapter XVI. Lucy discusses her reasons for her silence twice, telling us in different ways that silence gives her power.[11] When Lucy has been caught staring at Dr John/Graham, she says:

> I was confounded, as the reader may suppose, yet not with an irrecoverable confusion; being conscious that it was from no emotion of incautious admiration, nor yet in a spirit of unjustifiable inquisitiveness, that I had incurred this reproof. I might have cleared myself on the spot, but would not. I did not speak. I was not in the habit of speaking to him. Suffering him, then, to think what he chose, and accuse me of what he would, I resumed some work I had dropped, and kept my head bent over it during the remainder of his stay. There is a perverse mood of the mind which is rather soothed than irritated by misconstruction; and in quarters where we can never be rightly known, we take pleasure, I think, in being consummately ignored. What honest man on being casually taken for a housebreaker, does not feel rather tickled than vexed at the mistaking?
>
> (ch. X)

Lucy describes here a negative control that she exerts over the situation by not speaking. The syntax reveals an interesting mixture of actual passives ('confounded'), forms with passive connotations ('incurred', *being conscious* that it was from no emotion of *incautious admiration*, nor yet in a *spirit of unjustifiable* inquisitiveness [emphasis added]'), and declaratives ('I did not speak'). The picture is a clear one: rather than face his glance, she leans over her work and allows his rebuke to roll off her back. Suffering, she assumes control of herself and him by resuming her work.

There are several ways in which Lucy gains ascendance over the situation by not speaking. First, lacking the power to make John know her, she has the ability to make his ignorance of her her choice by withholding information. Thus, she transforms her disadvantage to an advantage by not sharing her knowledge. She prefers silence, her habit with Dr John, because she would rather continue to be ignored than claim the friendship that she is entitled to on the basis of old times. If Graham will not recognise her spontaneously or like her for herself, then she would just as soon not be known at all. Second, since she has a proper claim to John's attention, she puts herself above him by not making it: she seemingly martyrs herself to his insensitivity. Thus, her duplicity gains her a moral edge. Third, she appears to us as his superior since she 'rightly' knows him while she is certain that he will never 'rightly' know her. Finally, she gets a revealing pleasure from the deceit. As if tired of being the good girl, she says she derives perverse satisfaction from being thought bold. Significantly, she imagines herself an 'honest man', who can thus be (mistaken for) a housebreaker – criminal, daring, breaking the bounds of the house. The pleasure is partly in the ironic disparity between herself (the 'honest man') and the image of herself (the housebreaker), but partly in her momentary ability to play that role.

What she has actually broken are a series of gender, class and narrative conventions: by gazing at Dr John, she has acted like a man and an equal, not like a woman who inhabits the nursery; by keeping quiet, she has broken her covenant with us. We and John are both caught short by this reticence of hers. When Lucy reveals herself to him and us (that is, when she reveals to the reader that she has recognised him, and consequently enables us to recognise him), she tells us more about how denial confers power:

> I first recognised him on that occasion, noted several chapters back when my unguardedly-fixed attention had drawn on me the mortification of an implied rebuke. Subsequent observation confirmed in every point that early surmise. . . . To *say* anything on the subject, to *hint* at discovery, had not suited my habits of thought, or assimilated with my system of feeling. I liked entering his presence covered with a cloud he had not seen through, while he stood before me under a ray of special illumination.
>
> (ch. XVI)

Certain elements are continued from the first description of the scene – the 'implied rebuke' suggests the 'incurred reproof' and she refers again to her habits – but the power conferred is even more clearly stated. That Lucy is power*less* is marked by the 'mortification of an implied rebuke'; this rebuke was not important in the first telling of the episode – rather, there she seemed to enjoy travelling incognito, masquerading as a malefactor. Now she tells us that she was mortified. But she redresses that balance and gives herself an advantage with her strategy of knowing Dr John when he does not know her – he stands in the light, while she observes him from the shadows. He has the same inferior powers of perception as before, since he has not seen through her cloud, while he is totally illuminated for her. As cops in a '30s film conduct their interrogations with a spotlight on the suspect, so Lucy Snowe puts herself in a position of power by remaining in the dark.

But we must at the same time recognise that this is a defensive strategy; Lucy cultivates invisibility as she cultivates reason, to protect herself from pain.[12] And as a woman without property, she has little choice. On another occasion Lucy takes us into her confidence as to why she does not object to Mme Beck's prying; the truth is that she avoids a rupture in their relations that would most certainly result from a confrontation. But to understand that avoidance, we must remember that Lucy Snowe is financially dependent on Madame (ch. XIII). Because of her gender and status, she is limited in her direct access to power. So, she says: 'Well I knew that to him it could make little difference were I to come forward and announce "This is Lucy Snowe!" So I kept back in my teacher's place . . .' To be put down because of her position is preferable to being put down because of who she is. She may gain some power or self-esteem from the self-conscious adoption of a role that may have been enjoined on one by others.[13]

Does Lucy deceive her readers for the same reasons that she misleads characters within the novel? If that is so, what power does she gain? Just as her material in her dealings with the characters in the novel is information about herself, so in her dealings with the reader, her only material is her biography, which she can either give or withhold. Brontë employs a narrator who claims to be telling the true story of her life; her power depends on her ability to interest us in it. We are much more aware, however, of the power of language when it deceives us or leads us astray. The possibility of a straightforward referentiality in language is, of course, highly suspect these days; even to narrate the events in strict chronological order would be artful and full of rhetorical choices, but when language is used conventionally, it may *appear* to be transparent, merely reflecting the world of objects and emotions. When games are played with what is told us, however, we are much more conscious of the medium of the tale, and consequently of the authority of the teller.[14] Brontë can underline the assertion of that power by having her narrator deceive us and then undeceive us.

Another deception reveals the uses to which the strategy may be put. While Lucy is watching Mme Beck looking through her possessions, she mentions a bouquet of white violets, given to her by a 'stranger (a stranger to me, for we had never exchanged words)' (ch. XIII). In fact, M. Paul, who was not a stranger to us or to her, except in her definition, had given them to her.[15] Paul's lengthy reference to the flowers (ch. XXXI) and Lucy's pointed definition of stranger underscore the deception. What's going on here? First, Lucy effectively denies us knowledge of her. In particular, the flowers are a sign of M. Paul's interest in her, but we are left ignorant of this potential admirer. In terms of the plot, Brontë compels us to follow the relationship with John to its conclusion; in terms of character, she compels us to subscribe to a certain picture of Lucy. At the same time that she is disclaiming any lovers, she possesses flowers that could well have come from one. In revising the events to suit the needs of her narrative, she eliminates a possible source of strength. She may be making herself appear more vulnerable than she actually is, or alternatively she may be playing down the romantic attachment to Paul while she develops their friendship in preparation for a new definition of love.

Like the flowers, the passionate side of Lucy's character is hidden from the reader for some time. And this too is part of the narrator's control over us. Lucy presents herself at the beginning as simply calm, cowardly, slothful.[16] But that characterisation, like her preference for shadows, is not unequivocal. When Dr John insists on seeing her as quiet Lucy Snowe (ch. XXVI), she and we are aware of the inadequacy of that view. By that time we know that her calm and reasonable exterior is maintained only by constant struggle with her passionate core. Allowing individuals to make of her what they will (ch. XXVI), she retains her sense of superiority ('I smiled at them all'); allowing them to think little of her, she retains her privacy in a novel where there is much isolation but little of that valuable commodity. To a more limited extent, she does the same thing to her reader.

Lucy's relationship to women's speech is similarly ambivalent yet presented singly. She portrays herself as an observer, who is supposedly silent and isolated; she despises women like Ginevra who talk too much and praises Paulina's silence (ch. XXV), which is like her own. Yet, she has written the book we are reading, and controlled use of language is important to her throughout. For instance, she wants to impress her students with her language and regrets that her poor spoken French obstructs her domination of the classroom. But she can use sarcasm well enough in her own language, as we see when she silences Ginevra on the subject of John Bretton by describing a scene that never occurred. In that instance, she prefers the sense of power gained by saying one thing and meaning another, even though she might better have humiliated Ginevra by telling the truth (ch. XXI). In other words, by changing events she can exercise her control in a way that she could not by merely recounting them.

Control over language is, thus, underlined by the deceptive use of language; this mis-use is a way for the powerless to take power, and is a clue to the ethical gain accruing from this particular narrative strategy. At Lucy's nadir of strength, she seeks solace in the confessional. When John Graham Bretton questions her about the peculiar adventure which ended with Père Silas calling on him and bringing her to his door, she reassures him by saying that what she had said was 'no narrative', that her life had 'not been active enough for any dark deed, either of romance or reality' (ch. XVII). Lucy's theory of art expressed here suggests that only a particular kind of life (one full of activity and dark deeds) can be made into a narration. But her disclaimer to the contrary notwithstanding, she has been active, and she has narrated experiences exciting enough to interest the priest. Lucy was aware that she needed a friend or confidante; through speech, she is able to gain that for herself. Her response to her extreme isolation during the long vacation was to go out and tell her story to someone. In doing so, she won herself an ally who is responsible for bringing her back from her illness. Her text as a whole achieves that end for her with us – she is able to interest us in her by controlling the telling of her history. Narration as well as judicious silence, therefore, can allow a seemingly passive woman to act; if she cannot control her existence, she can at least control the telling of that existence.

II

The technique of withholding evidence then gives Lucy power over characters and audience. But this is not merely a text with a sometimes duplicitous narrator, but a text that is sometimes open. The two would seem to be in contradiction, since the openness appears to give the audience power: at two crucial junctures Lucy refuses to lead us, instead forcing us to imagine that her life has followed a typical pattern. In fact, however, this strategy fits with the other because she is still denying us information; although she empowers us to make up the story as we see fit, she still will not *tell* us what she knows. Let me cite both passages here. Lucy says the following about her late childhood:

> On quitting Bretton. . . . It will be conjectured that I was of course glad to return to the bosom of my kindred. Well, the amiable conjecture does no harm, and may therefore be safely left uncontra-

> dicted. Far from saying nay, indeed, I will permit the reader to picture
> me, for the next eight years, as a bark slumbering through halcyon
> weather, in a harbour still as glass. . . . A great many women and girls
> are supposed to pass their lives something in that fashion; why not I
> with the rest?
>   Picture me then idle, basking, plump, and happy. . . .
>
>   (ch. IV)

In the last paragraph but one of the novel, Lucy says this:

> Here pause: pause at once. There is enough said. Trouble no quiet,
> kind heart; leave sunny imaginations hope. Let it be theirs to conceive
> the delight of joy born again fresh out of great terror, the rapture of
> rescue from peril, the wondrous reprieve from dread, the fruition of
> return. Let them picture union and a happy succeeding life.

It would seem that the 'quiet, kind heart' and the 'sunny imagination'
are not overly insightful and are looked on with disdain for being
what they are. The seeming empowerment of the reader is related to
Lucy's tendency to lie because she judges us as she did Graham – if
we don't have the courage to imagine or tolerate the harsh truth, we
can improve things with hope. So we are back to chapter XVI: we
can see clearly as Lucy Snowe does, or through a cloud as John
Graham does.[17]

On both these occasions, as she refuses to tell us what the
beginning of her life was like, or how it ends for her, Lucy allows us
to imagine that she has led the life of other women, the heroines of
other novels. In this way the deceptiveness of the text and particularly
its openness are related to the substance of Lucy's life and to the plot
of the novel, for it is in the plot that we find the shape of Lucy's life
mirrored.[18] In other ways as well, Lucy is at pains to distinguish
herself from other women. For instance, she rejects the models
offered to her in the Museum; neither 'La Vie d'une femme' nor the
Cleopatra appeals to her. These pictures represent a reality represented elsewhere in the text: all too obviously, woman's lot is tied
up with and peripheral to the lives of men, and it is in this respect
that Lucy asserts that she is different. At the very moment that we are
permitted to imagine a non-existent happy past for Lucy, we are
called upon to envision a sad future for Polly ('How will she bear the
shocks and repulses, the humiliations and desolations, which books,
and my own reason, tell me are prepared for all flesh?' [ch. III]). In
the rest of the text, we find out of course that Polly has exactly the
placid life attributed to 'many women and girls'. While Lucy

experiences the shocks and desolations prepared imaginatively for Polly, Polly lives out the best of all the possible scenarios for attractive heterosexual women: true love leading to marriage. The other women in the novel are relentlessly focused on men, but without Polly's success: Mrs Bretton dotes on Graham; Miss Marchmont is a recluse mourning Frank; Ginevra Fanshawe must marry for money; the teachers at Mme Beck's school are engaged in intrigues. Lucy asserts that this lovesickness has nothing to do with her, assuming that the *billet doux* she has received was not intended for her:

> I did not dream it for a moment. Suitor or admirer my very thoughts had not conceived. All the teachers had dreams of some lover ... but into the realm of feelings and hope which such prospects open, my speculations, far less my presumptions, had never once had warrant to intrude.... I can't say that my experience tallied with theirs in this respect.
>
> (ch. XII)

Thus Lucy is aware that she is left out of the business of most women's lives because she is not attractive. (See for example chapter XXXIX where she disclaims any stake in the love based on beauty.)[19]

Brontë can do one of two things with this unattractive woman aware of her own lack. She can, as she does in *Jane Eyre*, show that looks are not everything and that clever and independent women possess virtues desired by men of insight and character. Or she can undermine the reader's desire for that sort of love. Her narrative strategy in *Villette* accomplishes both ends. We know that the current ending of the novel was in some sense dictated by Brontë's father; he wanted the novel to end with hero and heroine living happily ever after. The plot of the father, with its ideology of women's sexuality contained in marriage, is undercut, however, by its representation here. Instead of giving us one certain reading, Lucy gives us two ambiguous ones: Paul's drowning is never described, just a storm at sea. And the ending is meant to throw doubt on even that clarity. These gaps in her account are underscored because of the first-person narration. An outside voice could simply claim ignorance of what happened in those eight years or in the storm, but a first-person narrator cannot. Thus her decision can only be seen as a conscious resistance of the conventional 'happy ending'.[20]

But if Lucy is alone at the end, what are we to feel? Is it a triumph, escape from prison as Kate Millett would have it? Is it desperation or a life of cloistered mourning like that of Miss Marchmont? Looking at these narrative strategies we recognise that the power that Lucy has asserted throughout the recounting of her story is the power of denial; she has rebuffed Graham, Ginevra, and us at various times. Crucially, she rebuffs and teases M. Paul. In a strong parallel to the scene with Dr John, for instance, Lucy works on a bit of sewing while M. Paul lectures her; she withholds her present for him, enjoys angering him and is tickled by his idea that she is some rebel that must be kept down. When Lucy ceases to rebuff M. Paul, as she does when he shows her the school and his love, she is in danger of losing control and serving him instead as her king.

Throughout the novel, gifts have been an issue. For instance, Paul has given her books redolent of his masculine cigar and with the dangerous portions cut out; that is, through his gifts he has formed her mind in his own image of the proper woman. We learned from Lucy that Ginevra ought not to have accepted 'Isidore's' gifts if she did not mean to make him an equal gift of her regard. In this text, relations are seen to be systems of exchange, and there is a suggestion that Lucy would have to make a return on the school that Paul has established for her. 'I promised to do all he told me. I promised to work hard and willingly. "I will be your faithful steward. . . . I trust at your coming the account will be ready."' Since she cannot find words to express her meaning, she has recourse to action: 'I pressed it [his hand] close, I paid it tribute. He was my king; royal for me had been that hand's bounty; to offer homage was both a joy and a duty' (ch. XLI). She is a hostess for the first time and takes joy in tending M. Paul. Her working as a steward implies that the school is really his and that she could not have kept her independence in the presence of her beloved. Although he ceases to repress her when she most expects it (when she is jealous of his ward), that is because the jealousy reassures him that she is dependent upon him. M. Paul has to die, then, not to destroy Lucy Snowe but to prevent her taking second place to him.[21] If he were to come back, Brontë would not have succeeded in creating a new plot for a woman's life.

Despite the parallels suggested between Miss Marchmont and Lucy – the storms that overtake Frank and M. Paul, the similar characters of the two women – Lucy does not suffer the fate of her friend.[22] She is alone throughout the novel, at Bretton, at the Rue Fossette, but in the end she has a new kind of solitude, one that is founded on proprietorship and work. While at Mme Beck's she could sometimes be alone, she could never have privacy; because of her gender and economic position, she was subject to Mme Beck's surveillance. Paul has secured her privacy and taken her out from under that eye, but he does that so that their love can thrive. Lucy, however, adds to and extends her establishment for her own sake.

Lucy tells us that the three years that Paul was away were the three happiest of her life, and points out to us the paradox involved. Brontë seems to realise that the paradox is that for women in heterosexual relations, in some ways you are better off alone.[23] Having already schooled herself to the superiority of friendship and companionship to romantic love, Lucy is in an excellent position to survive this loss. She is not shipwrecked by the storm, as she was at the end of her supposed 'halcyon youth', but rather through the strategy of denial, she has developed the strength of character necessary to live her life and narrate it in a new and challenging way.

From *The Journal of Narrative Technique*, 15:3 (Fall, 1985), 244– 55.

NOTES

[Though in some ways Nancy Rabinowitz shares Tony Tanner's view (see above) of Lucy's narrative as an act of survival, she is more concerned with the formal aspects of narrative. Consequently, where Tanner writes in terms of Lucy's challenge to reality, Rabinowitz discusses the novel in terms of its challenge to realism. Rabinowitz explicitly takes up Mary Jacobus's challenge to theorise rather than explain away 'the incoherencies and compromises, inconsistencies and dislocations in the novel' (see p. 138 below for Mary Jacobus's essay). Both critics agree that the novel transcends the bounds of the realistic form, although they differ in the degree of consciousness each attributes to the narrator. So, whereas Rabinowitz sees Lucy's narrative as the product of a consciously chosen strategy of evasion and control, Jacobus ascribes more to the workings of Lucy's unconscious and to an insufficiently repressed Romanticism in the tale. Ed.]

1. On the unreliability of the narrator, see Robert Martin, *The Accents of Persuasion* (New York, 1966), p. 149; Sandra Gilbert and Susan Gubar, *The Madwoman in the Attic* (New Haven, 1979), p. 419; Mary Jacobus, 'The Buried Letter: Feminism and Romanticism in *Villette*', in *Women Writing and Writing about Women*, ed. Mary Jacobus (London, 1979), p. 43; Helene Moglen, *The Self Conceived* (New York, 1976), p. 199. For a view of Lucy as reliable, see Brenda R. Silver, 'The Reflecting Reader in *Villette*', in *The Voyage In: Fictions of Female*

Development, ed. Elizabeth Abel, Marianne Hirsch, and Elizabeth Langland (Hanover and London, 1983), pp. 90–111 [Extracts from Sandra Gilbert and Susan Gubar, Mary Jacobus, Helen Moglen, and Brenda Silver are all reprinted in this volume. Ed.]

2. Barbara J. Baines, 'Villette, a Feminist Novel', *Victorian Institute Journal*, 5 (1976), 51–9; Carolyn V. Platt, 'How Feminist is *Villette?*', *Women and Literature*, 3 (1975), 16–27; Judith Plotz, ' "Potatoes in a Cellar": Charlotte Brontë's *Villette* and the Feminized Imagination', *Journal of Women's Studies in Literature*, 1 (1979), 74–87. The recent popularity of *Villette* with feminist critics can perhaps be attributed to Kate Millett's treatment of the novel in *Sexual Politics*. [See p. 32 above. Ed.]

3. Earl Knies, *The Art of Charlotte Brontë* (Athens, Ohio, 1969), calls the world of *Villette* more complex and ambiguous.

4. Helene Moglen, *The Self Conceived* (New York, 1976), p. 196.

5. Mary Jacobus, 'The Buried Letter: Feminism and Romanticism in *Villette*', p. 58.

6. Nancy K. Miller, 'Emphasis Added', *PMLA*, 96:1 (1981), 46. Brenda Silver also works with Miller's terminology.

7. Nancy Miller remarks that 'the plots of women's literature are not about "life" and solutions in any therapeutic sense, nor should they be. They are about the plots of literature itself, about the constraints the maxim places on rendering a female life in fiction' (ibid., p. 46). Mary Jacobus, 'The Question of Language: Men of Maxims and *The Mill on the Floss*', *Critical Inquiry*, 8 (1981), 207–22, sees Maggie as Eliot's sacrifice, through which the author becomes 'an interpreter of the exotic possibilities contained in mysterious sentences'. The death of Maggie makes it possible for 'the writer to come into being' (p. 216).

8. Sandra Gilbert and Susan Gubar, *The Madwoman in the Attic* (New Haven, 1979), p. 419.

9. Nancy Miller, 'Emphasis Added', p. 47.

10. I disagree with Silver on this crucial point, although I would agree with what she says about the reasons for Lucy's behaviour: 'critics fail to look at . . . the reality of the codes that discourage women from actively pursuing their own ends except through marriage, and the limited models for development and access to material support once they are denied the protection of family and friends' ('The Reflecting Reader in *Villette*', pp. 98–9).

11. Helen Moglen, *The Self Conceived* (New York, 1976), p. 211, relates the silence to rejection, vulnerability and unreliability, while Silver calls it self-preservation (ibid., pp. 101–2).

12. Mary Jacobus, 'The Buried Letter: Feminism and Romanticism in *Villette*', calls Lucy's invisibility a 'calculated deception – a blank screen on which others project their view of her' (p. 231). Moglen [above] sees that she rejects because she fears rejection (p. 196).

13. In her discussion of Eliot and Irigaray, Jacobus says 'Her answer is "mimetism", the role historically assigned to women – that of reproduction, but deliberately assumed; an acting out or role playing with the text allows the woman writer the better to know and hence to expose what she mimics' ('The Question of Language', *Critical Inquiry*, 8 [1981], 40).

14. The gaps in the chronology are a part of the peculiar structure of this novel; they have been noted by others such as Karl Kroeber, *Styles in Fictional Structure* (Princeton, 1971), who contrasts Brontë's metaphoric language with Austen's more transparent style (p. 156), and asserts that Lucy Snowe is 'defined in part by her idiosyncratic distortions of normal sequence' (p. 161). Lucy's defiance of realistic norms may be seen in these breaks with chronological order (see Elizabeth Deeds Ermarth, *Realism and Consensus in the English Novel* [Princeton, 1983], and her earlier essay on the ways in which that consensus excludes women, 'Fictional Consensus and Female Casualties', in *The Representation of Women in Fiction*, ed. Carolyn G. Heilbrun and Margaret R. Higonnet [Baltimore, 1981], pp. 1–18).

15. Cf. Jean F. Blackall, 'Point of View *Villette*', *Journal of Narrative Technique*, 6 (1976), 14–28. She thinks that Lucy is the last to know that Paul loves her, and as a 'reminiscent narrator does not anticipate her own discovery for the reader. I think that Charlotte Brontë was both savouring a joke and fulfilling that self-important allegiance to realistic representation characteristic of her attitude toward fiction' (p. 24).

16. See, among others, Margot Horne, 'Portrait of the Artist as a Young Woman: The Dualism of Heroine and Anti-Heroine in *Villette*', *Dutch Quarterly Review*, 6, 216.

17. Rachel Brownstein, *Becoming a Heroine* (New York, 1982), p. 181.

18. Charles Burkhart, 'The Nuns of *Villette*', *Victorian Newsletter*, 44 (1973), 8–13, calls the following the question of the novel: 'Will she enter into life, like her friend the brilliant and demure Paulina, or retire from it, like ... Miss Marchont?' (p. 9). Gilbert and Gubar see Lucy Snowe doubled in the other characters of the novel, as do Moglen and Jacobus to a certain extent.

19. I take issue here with Jacobus' statement that Brontë is 'silent about the true nature and origin of Lucy's oppression' ('The Buried Letter', p. 233); I think that *Villette* does question the 'enshrining of marriage within Victorian sexual ideology' and 'its economic and social consequences for women'.

20. Judith L. Newton, *Women, Power and Subversion* (Georgia, 1981), remarks that Paul is sacrificed to Charlotte Brontë's sense of possibilities; the combination of love and quest is too good to be true (p. 124). See also Jean R. Kennard, *Victims of Convention* (Hamden, Conn., 1978), p. 106. Moglen (*The Self Conceived*, pp. 227–9) makes a psychological interpretation based on Brontë's own experience, but also recognises that 'for Lucy to be certain of keeping that independence, she would have to pay the price of solitude' (p. 228).

21. Robert Martin accepts the love plot as paramount, but cites 'a heavily facetious letter to George Smith [in which] Miss Brontë indicates that drowning would be a happier fate for Paul than marriage to "that-person-that-that-individual – Lucy Snowe"' (*The Accents of Persuasion* [New York, 1966], p. 186).

22. Martin (ibid., p. 152), sees the analogy as complete.

23. Charles Burkhart comments on the 'drift to solitude' ('The Nuns of *Villette*', *Victorian Newsletter*, 44 [1973], 9). The other alternative is to see Lucy amidst a community of women, but given her ambivalence toward other women, it is hard for me to imagine this. For another position, see Nina Auerbach, *Communities of Women* (Cambridge, Mass., 1978).

6

The Reflecting Reader in 'Villette'

BRENDA SILVER

'Who *are* you, Miss Snowe?' Ginevra Fanshawe asks the narrator-protagonist of Charlotte Brontë's *Villette*, a question echoed by generations of readers and critics and encouraged by Lucy Snowe herself.[1] An orphan, an outsider, a woman without family or country, an 'inoffensive shadow', and a ray so hot that at least one person shields his eyes from it – Lucy both courts and laments the roles assigned to her by others in what is rightfully read as her search for selfhood. Ultimately, however, *who* Lucy is is inseparable from *what* she is: a teller of tales unspeakable in the presence of either her comfortable and comforting godmother and the friends who surround her at La Terrasse, or the colder, more worldly, yet equally uncomprehending eavesdroppers at the pensionnat on the Rue Fossette. If, as has been argued, the 'reality' of a narrative is a mutual creation of the text and its readers, and this act depends on the author's ability to stimulate the imagination in such a way as to make us think in terms different from our own,[2] then Lucy, as if aware of this relationship, has self-consciously structured her use of silence and revelation to immerse us in a world as complex and conflicted as that which she herself experienced. Knowing, however, that she cannot trust others to perceive her as she is – that even when she is not invisible she is more than likely to be misread – Lucy goes one step further: she projects her readers into the landscape of the novel, the text, and asks them to use their imaginations in a mutual act of creation which in turn validates her own emerging self. In this way her narrative both inscribes her evolving identity and establishes a community of readers whose recognition and acceptance provide the context necessary for an individual's growth to maturity – a context all too often denied to women.

Although several critics have recently explored the role of Lucy's narration in the discovery and creation of her identity, most have assumed that she is an 'unreliable' narrator whose voice, according to Helene Moglen, is characterised by 'indirection' and 'neurotic rationalisation', and whose form for the novel is 'the form of [her] neurosis: a representation of the novel's subject'.[3] Mary Jacobus is more direct: 'Lucy lies to us. Her deliberate ruses, omissions and falsifications break the unwritten contract of first-person narrative (the confidence between reader and "I") and unsettle our faith in the reliability of the text.'[4] Gilbert and Gubar, on the other hand, accept Lucy's narrative reticence and evasions, her apparent attempts to mislead the reader, and attribute her 'anxious and guilty' feelings about her narrative to the fact that her 'life, her sense of herself, does not conform to the literary or social stereotypes provided by her culture to define and circumscribe female life'. The result is nothing less than a 'mythic undertaking – an attempt to create an adequate fiction of her own'.[5]

But it can also be argued that Lucy is less evasive and even less unreliable than most critics have assumed – that she is, in fact, a self-consciously reliable narrator of unusual circumstances whose narrative choices ask her 'readers' to perceive her on her own terms.[6] The difficulty may be that Lucy's terms are so different from the maxims and prejudices of the culture she inhabits and portrays that they are read by even sympathetic readers as perverse or implausible. Here I am borrowing the term and the concept of 'implausibility' put forward by Nancy Miller in her essay 'Emphasis Added: Plots and Plausibilities in Women's Fiction'.[7] In this piece, Miller defines the persistent misreading of women's texts as extravagant, implausible, unmotivated, or unconvincing in terms of the reader's expectations of what a narrative should be, and illustrates how these expectations are in turn determined or judged according to the dominant cultural ideology. Taking Gérard Genette's analysis of 'Vraisemblance et Motivation' as her starting point, Miller cites Genette's distinction between three different forms of narratives: the 'plausible narrative', which implicitly and silently obeys the conventions of genre and the cultural maxims on which they rest; the 'arbitrary narrative', which deliberately and silently destroys this collusion but refuses to justify itself; and the narrative with 'a motivated and "*artificial plausi-bility*"'. The last type, 'exemplified by the "endless chatting" of a Balzacian novel, we might call "other-directed", for here authorial commentary justifies its story to society by providing the missing maxims, or by inventing them' (pp. 38-9). As Miller points out, however, glossing Genette's analysis, what might *seem* to be silent or even absent in the arbitrary narrative – that is, an alternate set of maxims – 'may simply be inaudible to the dominant mode of reception' (p. 39).

Within this framework, Lucy's tale employs characteristics of both the artificially plausible narrative and the seemingly arbitrary narra-tive that in fact inscribes an alternative ideology, and both these narrative modes are encoded in her dialogue with the reader. Her constant shifting between self-justification and 'silence' thus becomes a plausible portrayal of the conflicting needs and desires she con-fronts and experiences without being able to count on either the ear or the understanding of those who dictate social behaviour – and plots of novels. Rather than misleading or lying to us, or to herself, Lucy is deliberately creating not only a new form of fiction for women, but a new audience – part critic, part confidante, part sounding board – whose willingness to enter her world and interpret her text will provide the recognition denied to women who do not follow traditional paths of development.

In order to test this hypothesis, we must trace Lucy's relationship to the fictionalised reader in the text, the created recipient of her tale. There are, in fact, particularly in the beginning of the novel, at least two readers to whom Lucy reveals different aspects of her experience and herself, in order to justify them to her critics or to confide them to a sympathetic listener. Later, as the narrative and Lucy's sense of herself evolve, the reader develops into an audience so accustomed to and accepting of Lucy's 'strange stammerings' (ch. 36), that the different readers are merged into one.

A similar development in the nature of the audience might also explain the ambiguity that informs our perception of the reader's gender. Although most readers today, I suspect, automatically think of the fictionalised reader addressed by Lucy as female, on the rare occasions that Lucy refers to her reader by pronoun, she uses the generic 'he' and 'his' (chs 8, 29, 30). In addition to following an accepted literary convention (and despite the fact that most novel readers were women), Lucy may deliberately be positing a male audience to emphasise that the power to pass both literary and moral judgements on her story belonged, in the public sphere, predominantly to men. Lucy's narrative choice here reflects her creator's experience in one such forum – critical reviews – where she had already suffered the pain of being labelled unconventional, unchristian, unfeminine and unsexed. That the harshest judgements came from other women, writing anonymously, highlights the force that social maxims exert on women's self-perceptions and the complexity of gender identification for unconventional women – and women writers.[8]

In her presentation of herself to others, then, Lucy is trebly constrained: as woman, as heroine, and as storyteller. From this perspective, the split between the two readers in the early part of Lucy's narrative may well signify a split between those readers who accept the cultural maxims about women in a patriarchy and want to find them mirrored in novels – an audience that speaks with a male voice and male authority and might well condemn her actions – and those readers, similar to the female personifications who populate Lucy's psychic landscape, in whom she can confide.[9] If this distinction breaks down later in the novel when the different readers begin to merge, it may be owing to Lucy's sense that she has so shaped her audience to her own ends that gender becomes insignificant.

In the beginning of her narrative, however, the entity whom Lucy addresses explicitly as 'reader' stands at a distance from Lucy herself in a potentially antagonistic posture. This reader first appears in her description of the eight years that intervene between the visit to Bretton described in the early chapters and the events that leave her on her own without family or support. 'I will permit the reader', she writes, 'to picture me ... as a bark slumbering through halcyon weather, in a harbour still as glass – the steersman stretched on the little deck, his face up to heaven, his eyes closed: buried if you will in a long prayer' – the situation in which 'a great many women and girls are supposed to pass their lives' (ch. 4). The identification of the reader here with the way things are supposed to be – with the conventional expectations for women's lives – makes this reader the exponent of truisms about women that Lucy knows from her own experience are not valid. The irony of her 'permission' to her readers to deceive themselves emphasises society's refusal to see or to admit the actual circumstances of her – and by implication other women's – existence. The result of this refusal is to invalidate Lucy's perception of her own reality, and to make Lucy herself invisible.

From society's perspective, then, Lucy has no being, and her subsequent presentation of herself as a shadow, as well as other characters' misreading of her nature and her needs, mirrors her social reality.

Lucy's insight into the disparity between social expectations and reality for women, however, clashes throughout the novel with her simultaneous awareness that she has internalised the very maxims that restrict her development by their failure to recognise her existence. Not only does she lack a blueprint for her journey to selfhood – that is, a conventional plot – but she envisions and presents herself as a divided being whose strengths and weaknesses, as well as her economic and emotional needs, are continually at odds with each other. Forced by circumstances into self-reliance and exertion, denied the luxury of remaining in the prayerful sleep assumed of women, she struggles to compromise between her necessarily unconventional actions and her need to remain within the social structure. As Lucy herself tells us, early in life she developed 'a staid manner of my own which ere now had been as good to me as cloak and hood of hodden grey; since under its favour I had been enabled to achieve with impunity, and even approbation, deeds that, if attempted with an excited and unsettled air, would in some minds have stamped me as a dreamer and zealot' (ch. 5).

Coming at the moment of her decision to go to London, this statement inscribes the parameters of Lucy's social and narrative stance: her realism and her rebellion. Her cloak of staidness ensures her the acceptance and help not only of Mrs Barrett, her old nurse, but of the old waiter at the London inn who becomes the first of her many guides. Later, it secures her the approval of Madame Beck and the Count de Bossompierre, also enabling figures, and prevents others from detecting her love for Graham or Paul. But this cloak also masks her other self: the woman who chafes at her restrictions, even while apologising for her pleasure in walking around London by herself or being rowed through the night to the boat that will carry her over the Channel. And nowhere is this conflict clearer than in her dialogue with her two readers at the onset of her journey: the conventional or socialised reader, who embodies society's maxims about women and whom she creates to ask the implied questions and make the implied criticisms she anticipates in her relation with the world; and the rebellious or unsocialised reader, in whom she confides those perceptions and feelings so far removed from the social conventions as to have little or no plausibility if uttered aloud.

If, in her justification of her actions to the socialised reader, she self-consciously creates an 'artificially plausible' narrative, the dialogue with the rebellious reader assumes a shared perspective – an arbitrary narrative – that gradually dominates both readers and informs the text.

Before tracing the evolution of her two readers, however, we must examine the circumstances that force Lucy to create her own life. By the time we meet her at Bretton, all the seeds of the disaster that starts her upon her journey have already been sown, and she herself has begun to develop the social and narrative stances that become more pronounced later on. The most significant factor is, of course, her solitude. Residing with unidentified kinfolk, picturing her stay at Bretton as a period of calm in a pilgrim's progress, Lucy has already acquired a sense of herself as an outsider, an observer rather than an actor, who is capable of telling Polly that she must learn to hide her feelings and not expect too much from others. This restraint is particularly necessary, she implies, in the situation that prompts her remark: the unequal power relationship that exists between young men such as Graham, her god-brother, who go to school and visit friends, and the girls who sit at home reading and sewing and waiting for them.

Although Polly's role as Lucy's psychological double is well established, Kate Millett's cultural interpretation of this doubling is worth noting here: 'Brontë keeps breaking people into two parts so we can see their divided and conflicting emotions; [Polly] is the worshipful sister, Lucy the envious one. Together they represent the situation of the girl in the family'[10] – the situation, we might add, of a younger sister in a family with an adored son. Under these circumstances, the sister/girl might, like Polly, choose to serve the idol; or she might resent the privilege and desire, however unconsciously, the power for herself. Lucy, even at this age, is divided between the two responses, but she does refuse to play Polly's role, and this choice inevitably increases her isolation. Instead, she adopts the protective facade of coolness, calm and quiet that serves both to confine her conflicting desires and mask her rebellion.

Nowhere, perhaps, are the effects of Lucy's solitude more evident than in the loss of social status that accompanies her loss of family, a clear indication of the interconnected role of class and gender in determining a person's development – and worth. Denied the material support and visibility traditionally provided by father, husband, or kin, and denied the education that men of her class usually received, she had few if any options open to her that would not further her alienation from her class or prevent her from following the acceptable routes for female development: marriage or death. We have only to contrast the course of Graham's life after his family suffers a financial setback to Lucy's to see vividly the obstacles working against her growth. Both, as Lucy unequivocally states, began life in the same social station.[11] But whereas Graham enters his father's profession, medicine, and by virtue of it moves out into the world and up the social ladder – not to mention his support of his mother – Lucy withdraws into the two hot closed rooms of Miss Marchmont's house before crossing the Channel to enter the conventual environment and enclosed garden of the Rue Fossette. The perils of her friendless and solitary state are graphically illustrated upon her arrival in Villette, when she not only has to ask the now lordly Graham to speak for her and suggest an inn, but, once separated from him, becomes the victim of male pursuit and harassment.

If these 'respectable' men perceive Lucy, the solitary streetwalker, as a prostitute, they are only assigning to her the role often assumed by women left in her position – a role simultaneously recognised and outlawed by society. Lucy chooses another path. In leaving England to seek work as a governess/teacher, she adopts one of the few means of support available to embarrassed gentlewomen, but this choice also forces her to 'admit the realities of her status as a paid employee and resign herself to the loss of her place in English society'.[12] However exhilarated Lucy may be walking around London or aboard ship, she realises only too well that her loss of status will prevent her from achieving what women were expected to desire – marriage with an equal or superior and the protection that such a union would offer her. Denied the wealth, position, or beauty that would make her a desirable object of possession, she will be unable to overcome the inequality inherent in the relationship between supposedly passive women and successful young men such as Graham. Although Lucy is clear-sighted enough to perceive that she does not have the means to play the traditional female roles enacted by other women in the novel – Ginevra, Paulina, or Mrs Bretton – the desires she represses haunt her still. They surface both in her poignant questions to Paul at the end of the novel: 'Ah, I am not pleasant to look at –?' and 'Do I displease your eyes *much?*' (ch. 41); and in her yearning to assume woman's most traditional role by becoming, in her words, one of those who 'lay down the whole burden of human egotism, and gloriously take up the nobler charge of labouring and living for others' (ch. 31).

The conflict between Lucy's acknowledgement of her social position and the emotional needs that she has internalised (a conflict that
is reflected in her creation of the two readers), is further complicated
by her unfeminine desire to be her own person – to achieve
independence – and her knowledge of her powers: an active intellect
and the ability to feel strongly and act decisively. When Ginevra,
observant in her own worldly way, defines Lucy during their mirror
scene after the play by declaring 'Nobody in the world but you cares
for cleverness' (ch. 14), she simultaneously acknowledges one of
Lucy's strongest attributes and reflects its lack of value in the context
of cultural expectations for women. Early in the novel, Lucy
measures her pride of intellect (and it is great) against the transformation into a beautiful wife and mother she observes in a less
intelligent woman who had been at school with her. Intelligence, she
perceives, does not lead to social visibility or acceptance: she
recognises the older woman but is not in turn recognised by her. The
language of this scene captures Lucy's conflicting self-definitions and
her characteristic response: 'Wifehood and maternity had changed
her thus, as I have since seen them change others even less promising
than she. Me she had forgotten. [The 'she' here is ambiguous:
wifehood and motherhood, or the woman? Both, I would say.] I was
changed, too, though not, I fear, for the better. I made no attempt to
recall myself to her memory: why should I?' (ch. 5). Why indeed!
    Lucy partly resolves the conflict between intelligence and woman-
hood by insisting throughout the novel that *others* perceive her as
clever, or interested in learning, or quick, whereas in truth she was
none of these things. In much the same way, she justifies to the reader
her major decision to go forward into the classroom (rather than
backward into the nursery) as a reaction to what she describes as
Madame Beck's masculine challenge to her gifts. A closer look,
however, reveals that through this 'justification' she transforms what
appears to be an arbitrary personal choice into an assertion of female
selfhood broad enough to include intellectual ambition and achievement. She creates, that is, a plausible social and narrative context for
her own self-development that in turn opens the way for other
women to follow her. Later, goaded into intellectual activity by Paul,
she declares: 'Whatever my powers – feminine or the contrary – God
had given them, and I felt resolute to be ashamed of no faculty of His
bestowal' (ch. 30).
    The power of conflicting cultural maxims revealed by Lucy's
seeming denial of her own strengths manifests itself in linguistic as

well as psychological evasions. Forced by her situation to speak as well as to act for herself, she adopts speech patterns that allow her simultaneously to justify her actions – both to society and to herself – and to mask their true import. The most striking of these is her well-documented presentation of herself as acted on, an object, rather than as actor, the subject or agent of the sentence or the deed. At every turning point in the novel, at every moment of decision, Lucy chooses instinctively to break free of social constraints and go forward to self-discovery and growth, even while denying that the decision or action is hers. 'Fate', she writes, 'took me in her strong hand' and directed her to knock at the door of the pensionnat; 'a bold thought' – to go to London – 'was sent to my mind; my mind was made strong to receive it' (chs 7, 5). Further complicating her self-presentation is her clear sense of what she is and is not, of what she will or will not do, a certainty that often masks itself in the grammatical construction, 'it did not suit me'. Later, however, as Lucy begins to gain confidence and a sympathetic audience, her assertions of herself as agent, 'I', rather than object, 'me', become more frequent; but she continues to the end to insist that other people or changed circumstances guide her and are responsible for her economic and social success.

While many critics have offered explanations for what Moglen calls Lucy's 'language of passivity', they often fail to look at what I have been emphasising: the reality of the codes that discourage women from actively pursuing their own ends except through marriage, and the limited models for development and access to material support once they are denied the protection of family and friends.[13] The problem of voice illustrated by Lucy's difficulty in saying 'I' reflects her isolation within a culture that rejects her strengths for lack of a context in which to read them – the same isolation that forces her to create her own readers. In her conversation with Graham about the illness induced by her solitude, Graham's question '"Who is in the wrong, then, Lucy?"' evokes the response, '"Me – Dr John – me; and a great abstraction . . . me and Fate"' (ch. 17). Fate here becomes the ironic embodiment of those circumstances that Lucy knows better than to speak aloud, even if she had the words to describe them, since they lack the social recognition or cultural context that would make her narration of them plausible. In fact, society itself is at a loss for words when describing Lucy's state, just as Dr John is at a loss to prescribe anything to cure her. His suggestions for her future care – change of air and scene, cheerful society, exercise – may bear, as Lucy comments in one of her classic understatements, 'the safe sanction of custom, and the well-worn stamp of use' (ch. 17), but they fail utterly to recognise how inimical 'custom' and 'use' are to women in Lucy's uncustomary situation. For custom and use are exactly those forces that move Lucy to justify her tremendous delight in walking around London alone, frown on her unaccompanied journey to Boue-Marine where she is the only woman in the hotel breakfast room, permit respectable men to pursue a solitary woman across town for their sport, and ultimately imprison her alone in the school during the vacation. Lucy's 'bad grammar', then, her 'me', accurately captures the way custom and use blind society to the reality of lives like Lucy's and reduce women to objects.

Yet another interpretation of Lucy's language of passivity is made possible by Miller's analysis of how psychology and fiction have supported the customary reading of women's ambitions and desires as erotic or romantic, thereby severely limiting their range of self-expression in either social discourse or daydreams. Quoting Freud's statement – ' "In young women erotic wishes dominate the phanta-sies almost exclusively, for their ambition is generally comprised in their erotic longings; in young men egoistic and ambitious wishes assert themselves plainly enough alongside their erotic desires" ' (p. 40) – Miller finds in women's novels a challenge to this restrictive view, finds another economy: 'In this economy, egoistic desires would assert themselves paratactically alongside erotic ones. The repressed content, I think, would be, not erotic impulses, but an impulse to power: a fantasy of power that would revise the social grammar in which women are never defined as subjects; a fantasy of power that disdains a sexual exchange in which women can partici-pate only as objects of circulation' (p. 41). This power, however, will manifest itself as what it is – the power of the weak – and ' "the most essential form of accommodation for the weak is to conceal what power they do have" '.[14]

Lucy, then, must conceal in her discourse her supposedly masculine 'ambitious wishes' as well as her erotic desires, both of which forcefully assert themselves on the one occasion when she is em-powered by society to adopt the role of actor on the public stage. One of the most notable aspects of this scene, the school play, is its deliberate confusion of sex roles and gender identification. Cast as a man in a plot written by someone else, Lucy brilliantly enacts the initiative, the competitiveness, the courtship, the wit, and the power that in real life are denied her by her social status and her gender. As Graham says after the fact, she made 'a very killing fine gentleman' (ch. 16), and her first act, once in the role, is to conquer the duplicitous Zélie St Pierre by asserting the weakness of the latter's female sex.

Although Lucy does not want to *be* or to *win* the beautiful and self-confident Ginevra, the object of her desire within the fantasy/play, she clearly relishes the freedom to exercise her hidden powers. Her consciousness of this desire emerges in her acknowledged source of inspiration: the presence of Graham in the audience, the brother/rival who animated her to act 'as if wishful and resolute to win and conquer' and in the process to 'rival' and then 'eclipse' him (ch. 14). What Lucy also recognises, however, is that the roles men such as Graham play naturally by virtue of their gender, she can fill only by proxy, and her rejection of her faculty and relish for dramatic expression is in part a refusal to dissipate her energy on goals that she can achieve only by adding the tokens of manhood to her female self in the fantastic realm of the theatre. The self-respect implicit in her refusal to dress completely as a man for the role – to deny her femaleness – demands that her search for identity and fulfilment occurs on a different stage. For her, the audience at the play did not number 'personal friends and acquaintances'; 'foreigners and strangers', the crowd could not provide the recognition necessary for her growth (chs 15, 14).

Although Lucy rejects living by proxy (Ginevra's way) and refuses to perform before an audience of strangers, the play does allow her to test her powers and find her voice, an experience that informs her on-going dialogue with her chosen audience, the reader. 'Who will lend me a tongue?' she asks near the end of her tale, knowing only too well that she can rely on no one but herself. Her struggle to take control of her narrative (as well as of her life) is mirrored in the creation of an audience whose presence and responsiveness increasingly provide her with the strength to be that comes from external recognition. The complexity of her relationship with her readers and the changing roles she assigns to them as the narrative progresses reflect in turn the difficulty of growing to selfhood amidst the contradictory needs and desires imposed upon her by the prevailing cultural codes.

Even before she explicitly projects and names her readers, however, while still at Bretton, Lucy's awareness of the social and emotional forces shaping her identity colours her narrative presenta-

tion of herself. Early in the second chapter, for example, we read, 'I.
Lucy Snowe, plead guiltless of that curse, an over-heated and
discursive imagination', and we wonder to whom she is speaking and
why she talks of herself in this way. The implied listener, depicted as
judge and jury, is almost certainly a precursor of the conventiona
socialised reader before whom Lucy feels it necessary to disclaim the
passionate expression of emotion enacted by Polly, even while
implicitly admitting its power. Lucy names herself here by emphasising the cold aspect of her name as well as the light, names herself as
the plain, shy, dowerless girl who already perceives that emotions as
strong as those displayed by Polly may find no outlet in the world
created by her circumstances – and might well hinder her power to
survive.

Throughout the first part of the novel, Lucy continues to preserve
her self by distancing those emotions that threaten her precarious
economic and psychic equilibrium, particularly her feelings for
Graham. After a night of suffering, for example, caused by her bitter
knowledge that the romance Madame Beck suspects between her and
Dr John does not exist, the 'Next day', she tells us, she 'was Lucy
Snowe again' (ch. 13). A curious cross-over of roles between Polly
and Lucy, however, occurs in the one scene where Lucy does act out
her love for Graham – the night she loses his letter. '"Oh! they have
taken my letter'" cried the grovelling, groping monomaniac': this is
Lucy's depiction of herself (ch. 22). The phrase 'monomaniac' echoes
her previous description of Polly's attachment to her father as 'tha
monomaniac tendency I have ever thought the most unfortunate
with which man or woman can be cursed' (ch. 2). The teasing
response that Lucy's display of her feelings evokes in Graham makes
us feel that her refusal to declare her love to him (she acknowledges i
in a variety of ways to herself and her readers) is not neurotic, o
evasive, or even mistaken. Graham may guide her in her explorations
of her external environment from feelings of kindness or 'camaraderie'
but he will never perceive her inner life or fulfil her emotional needs
She observes him directly; he, as in the recognition scene in the
nursery, sees her in the mirror of his own egotism and therefore fail:
to see her at all. It is not surprising, then, that she justifies to the
reader her decision to conceal her identity from him by saying i
would have made little difference had she 'come forward and
[announced], "This is Lucy Snowe!"' (ch. 16).

Lucy's public silence and private dialogue with her reader are
deliberate responses to what is perhaps the most potentially destruc

tive aspect of her solitude: the isolation of vision that excludes her from the social discourse necessary for an ontological affirmation of self. However great her emotional self-discipline, Lucy realises early on the need to acknowledge and share her perceptions of reality in order to continue to be. Thus, she reacts to her observation of Polly at the Bretton tea table by confiding, 'Candidly speaking, I thought her a little busy body' (ch. 2). The as yet unnamed recipient of this confidence serves a crucial function both in the narrative and in Lucy's development, for no one actually present during that scene would have understood Lucy's rejection of Polly's exaggerated acting of the female role, just as no one at La Terrasse, including Mrs Bretton, 'could conceive' her suffering during the long vacation: 'so the half-drowned life-boatman [Lucy] keeps his own counsel, and spins no yarns' (ch. 17). Continually a confidante herself, a mediator who interprets the infant Polly's unspoken need to say goodbye to her cherished Graham and who later smooths the way to their union by speaking for them to Mr Home, Lucy, in her formative years, has no one to hear her unuttered words, or to speak in her place. The one exception is perhaps Miss Marchmont, who interprets Lucy's lack of words when confronted with an unorthodox question about suffering and salvation not as silence but encouragement (ch. 4). No wonder Lucy loves her, and after her death turns increasingly to the reader to fill the gap. Speak she must, though, for to remain silent would be to become the cretin who makes mouths instead of talking, and whose silence becomes a metaphor for Lucy's own potentially arrested development. To overcome this two-fold silence, Lucy evolves another reader, a nonjudgemental reader, a sharer of the insights that she cannot communicate to those more in tune with the accepted social codes.

When first left on her own, however, after the metaphoric shipwreck, Lucy's recognition of society's power to render her invisible and mute leads her initially to endow her newly created 'reader' with the conventional assumptions about women and novels that she must challenge and change for her own life and tale to be plausible. The irony evident in her first direct address to this reader ('I will permit the reader to picture me ... as a bark slumbering through halcyon weather ...') allows her simultaneously to mock those who choose to remain locked within their traditional expectations and to offer them an alternate version of reality that would reflect and validate her existence. This same ironic stance informs Lucy's care to keep the reader abreast of the chronological 'story' in her narrative, even as she manipulates the sequence and imagery to reveal a deeper stratum of her psychic life and the true meaning of her tale. 'Has the reader forgotten Miss Ginevra Fanshawe?' (ch. 9), she asks after she is well established as a teacher and as a prelude to the introduction of Dr John. The tinge of sarcasm in her question indicates that the perceptive reader will recognise the priorities implicit in the seemingly discontinuous narrative structure: the need for economic security – the effort of learning French and mastering a strange environment – far outweighed any other considerations in those early days. Later, the question 'Does the reader, remembering what was said some pages back, care to ask how I answered [Graham's] letters . . .?' (ch. 23) reminds both the curious reader and herself of her need to keep her emotions in check in the midst of the 'new creed . . . a belief in happiness' that she has just described.

Often, Lucy's mode in dealing with the reader is a form of cooptation that transforms the reader into an accomplice in whatever observation she is about to make: 'I need not explain, reader', or 'The reader will not be surprised', or 'My reader, I know, is one who would not thank me for an elaborate reproduction of poetic first impressions; and it is well, inasmuch as I had neither time nor mood to cherish such' (ch. 5). In this last address, she is undercutting romantic expectations as deliberately as she does when she rejects metaphors of buds and sylphs in describing the substantial young women of Villette (ch. 20) or tells us that 'M. Paul stooped down and proceeded – as novel-writers say, and, as was literally true in his case – to "hiss" into my ear some poignant words' (ch. 28). By mocking fictional and thereby social conventions, by challenging her readers to share her perceptions, she creates an audience who learns to read her narrative for what it is – the non-traditional story of a woman's life and a text in which she is not an invisible outsider but the informing presence.[15]

This dialogue, however, no matter how sarcastic it may be about conventions, also serves as self-protection and stems from Lucy's conflict between rebellious self-expression and survival. In this context, the reader becomes a foil whose role is to help her keep her own emotions in check. Thus, the irony in her early addresses is often directed as much toward herself as toward the social maxims she criticises; she uses it to curb her own imagination and desires when she feels them destructive of her precariously held security, or to define herself within the limits she recognises as realistic for someone in her position. When, after her romantic vision of Europe, she adds the postscript, 'Cancel the whole of that, if you please, reader – or rather let it stand and draw thence a moral ... *Day-dreams are delusions of the demon*' (ch. 6), she asserts the boundaries of what is possible in the battle she is then fighting for survival. When she makes comments such as 'The reader must not think too hardly of Rosine' (ch. 13) for chattering to Dr John, or 'Think not, reader, that [Ginevra] thus bloomed and sparkled for the mere sake of M. Paul' (ch. 14), the sarcasm aimed at these two women is also a way of confronting her own potentially self-destructive frustration at the fact that her position and personality prevent her from acting as freely as Rosine and Ginevra do. In the first of these examples, she is also levelling an ironic eye on her own tendency to idolise Dr John and the dangers of that idolisation. One of the most painful of these exchanges occurs at the time she is fighting her disappointment at the loss of Graham's attention: 'The reader will not too gravely regard the little circumstance that about this time' Madame Beck temporarily borrowed Graham's letters (ch. 26). The irony here is a self-protective reaction meant to distance the anger and pain that she is unable to allay except by containing them.

Rather than an attempt to deny the strength of her feelings or to deceive herself about them, as some critics have maintained, these passages speak to Lucy's recognition of the need to confront and control what she cannot realistically hope to gain or fulfil. To act out her emotional needs at this time might well threaten the economic and social security she achieves by ruthless, if painful, self-control. A revealing example of this struggle, and of her conscious involvement of the reader as a foil, occurs when Graham comes to take her to the theatre: 'And away I flew, never once checked, reader, by the thought which perhaps at this moment checks you: namely, that to go anywhere with Graham and without Mrs Bretton could be objection-able' (ch. 23). The fact is that 'society' might well look askance at this arrangement, except that society in the form of Mrs Bretton, as Lucy tells us immediately, sees their relationship as that of brother and sister. In the face of society's blindness to any other possibility, Lucy reacts by saying that she would feel self-contempt and shame for suggesting an intimacy that did not exist. In this exchange, the reader, as society's voice, is reassured that all is conventional and well. By now, however, Lucy has also trained her reader to hear and approve what is not stated explicitly: the consciously chosen res-traint that allows her to maintain the limited relationship offered her, and to benefit from it.

The dialogue with the reader, then, is both ironic and deadly serious, for Lucy's ability to retain her sense of her own integrity in spite of her invisibility and her conflicting needs is crucial for her growth. As the narrative (and with it Lucy's sense of selfhood) progresses, we can chart the nature of her development by the number and kind of addresses to her various readers. Not surprisingly, she appeals to her reader most often during times of intense self-conflict and when, owing to the lack of recognised context or precedent for her responses, she is least able to express herself openly. These moments occur both when she is alone and in social gatherings. Thus, left on her own, Lucy responds to the weight of her isolation ('To whom could I complain?') by deliberately rationalising and justifying to the socialised reader what are by conventional standards her unorthodox actions and feelings: 'In going to London, I ran less risk and evinced less enterprise than the reader may think' (ch. 5); 'Before you pronounce on the rashness of the proceeding, reader [her decision to go to Villette], look back to the point whence I started' (ch. 7). By combining irony and defensiveness, these early explanations constitute a critique of the codes she recognises as limiting even as they define her sense of self and her discourse. Although she gives the socialised reader permission to interpret her experience along traditional lines, she suffers from the potential misreading and its ability to control her life. The second address continues, 'consider the desert I had left, note how little I perilled: mine was the game where the player cannot lose and may win' – a clear indication of a conscious choice aimed at physical as well as psychic survival, and part of Lucy's challenge to the fiction that women pass their lives in a long sleep.

The nature of her addresses to the reader begins to change once Lucy is accepted into the foreign world of the pensionnat at the Rue Fossette. After her introduction to Madame Beck, she appeals to the reader four times in quick succession to share her confused reaction of admiration and shock at discovering a woman so powerful, so independent, so successful, and, in many ways, so like her! Simultaneously observed and observing, she gains the strength to offer a compelling portrait of this fascinating woman to the 'sensible reader' who will recognise that she did not gain 'all the knowledge here condensed for his benefit in one month, or in one half-year' (ch. 8). With Madame Beck's power – and eye – to stimulate her, she educates the reader as she herself learns of her ability to control her environment – and her tale.

Once she enters the classroom and immerses herself in teaching and learning ('My time was now well and profitably filled up. . . . It was pleasant. I felt I was getting on' [ch. 9]), her rare addresses to the reader are limited to ironic observations about Ginevra and Rosine, who play more traditional female roles, with the exception of the crucial scene when she refuses to tell Dr John – or the reader – why she is staring so intently at him: 'I was confounded, as the reader may suppose, yet not with an irrecoverable confusion; being conscious that it was from no emotion of incautious admiration. . . . I might have cleared myself on the spot, but would not. I did not speak. I was not in the habit of speaking to him' (ch. 10). He, as she has already told us, barely notices her existence. Her decision not to reveal herself where she 'can never be rightly known' has, not surprisingly, led to the strongest accusations of narrative unreliability, as well as accusations of lying, neurosis and perversity – the word she herself uses during this scene: 'There is a perverse mood of the mind which is rather soothed than irritated by misconstruction.' But is it not possible that by this silence Lucy is creating a script other than that in which the lost god-brother/prince reappears and rescues her from her changeling role, the romantic or erotic fantasy that Lucy finds it necessary to forgo while she makes an independent life for herself as a teacher? In terms of conventional fictions, she may be unreliable and her decision 'implausible', but in terms of the subtext, her silence and refusal reflect the lack of a language or a plot by which women can communicate ambitions and desires outside of those encoded in the accepted social or literary conventions. I am reminded here of Miller's appropriation of Jakobson's observation about communication: '"The verbal exchange, like every form of human relation, requires at least two interlocutors; an idiolect, in the final analysis, therefore can be only a *slightly perverse fiction*"' (p. 43). To transform Lucy's silence and refusal into a statement of alternative plausibility and action requires the participation of a reader willing to recognise and respond to her need for anonymity as part of her process of self-identification and growth.

Paradoxically, her silence initially gives Lucy power; under its protection she can observe and confront Graham's blindness toward Ginevra and plunge into the role of mediator in others' communications. She has begun the process that allows her, on the night of the play, to find her own voice. Left alone during the long vacation, however, she faces the 'dumb future' with a despair she no longer tries to hide from even her socialised readers (the religious reader, moralist, cynic, epicure) or to justify herself except by saying, 'perhaps, circumstanced like me, you [reader] would have been, like me, wrong' (ch. 15). The need for companionship, the need to speak, that drives her to the confessional at the height of her despair, becomes, once outside the church, a 'confession' to a reader whose by now sympathetic hearing she relies on when she rejects Père Silas's tempting offer of religious community and chooses instead to live her life as a 'heretic narrative' (ch. 15). In the scenes that follow this confession, she has ample opportunity to test the mettle of her now transformed reader/confessor, for her revelation to Graham that she is 'Lucy Snowe' plunges her into a deeper stratum of isolation than that she had experienced before she was 'known'. During her stay at La Terrasse and the subsequent weeks, when her self-control and clarity of vision are most sorely tried, she turns to the reader more often than at any other time during the narrative.[16] Most of her addresses obsessively explain what she calls the 'seeming inconsistency' of her portraits of Graham, an inconsistency that reflects her struggle to say honestly what she instinctively knows: that he is neither as perceptive nor sensitive nor selfless as he appears to others in public. Limited by his 'masculine self-love' and conventionality, lacking the necessary sympathy, he will never replace the reader as the sharer of Lucy's inner life.

The battle against self-delusion that Lucy fights during this section of the narrative with the explicit help of the reader reaches its climax in the 'Vashti' chapter. In fact, the five evocations of the reader during this chapter accurately inscribe the process of Lucy's self-recognition and growth. First, making use of an endearment that jars us coming from her usually more satiric pen, she shares with the 'dear reader' both the initial ecstasy that Graham's letters brought her and the mellowing effect that time and self-knowledge had on their message. Next, she reminds the reader of her compromise in answering the letters – a struggle in which reason vanquishes imagination, but at a price: the painful confession to the reader of why it was acceptable for her to go out alone with her 'brother' Graham. Immediately following this admission, she sees the light in the attic, indicative of the presence of the nun, which 'the reader may believe ... or not'. Graham's disbelief, however, causes Lucy to comment negatively on his 'dry, materialist views', views which colour his subsequent 'callous' reaction to Vashti, the passionate actress who enacts Lucy's own rebellion and self-mastery. Graham's 'branding judgement' impresses upon Lucy once and for ever his inability to perceive who or what she is. The final vision of Graham that she offers to the reader that night mirrors her acceptance of his separateness: 'Reader, I see him yet, with his look of comely courage and cordial calm' amidst the chaos released by Vashti's desires. He has become a statue, heroic perhaps, the ideal suitor for Polly, but not for Lucy a responsive human being.

After the period of solitary confinement and silence that follows this eventful night, Lucy returns to her dialogue with the reader stronger and calmer. She is now able to be warmly ironic and even humorous about the 'perverseness' that leads her to 'quarrel' with M. Paul (in contrast to her decision *not* to quarrel with Graham) and continues to define her distinctive emerging self. At least part of the change of tone – and the relative sparseness of the addresses to the reader she now speaks to without justification as a true companion – can be attributed to Paul, whose belief in her 'fiery and rash nature' (ch. 26) gives her a warmer image of her self and whose own perverseness badgers her into speaking to him directly. One scene deserves note: the evening at the Hotel Crécy when her open anger and forgiveness wins from M. Paul a smile that she presents to the reader as her own accomplishment ('You should have seen him smile, Reader, ...' [ch. 27]). Emphasising his contrast to Graham, this smile transforms Paul from a mask or a statue into a human being.

Unable, however, to trust Paul completely, Lucy continues to share with the reader the difficulties of the unfolding relationship and of the man: 'the reader is advised not to be in any hurry with his kindly conclusions' (ch. 30). Most significant, perhaps, she alludes again and again to the 'perverse' aspect of her character that now prevents her from succumbing to Paul's 'Est-ce là tout?' or remaining in the classroom when he seeks her on the evening after the country outing during which he had called her 'sister' and encouraged her love (chs 29, 33). This behaviour suggests that Lucy is experiencing a poten-tially irresolvable conflict between her long-concealed erotic desires and her supposedly masculine ambitious wishes. On the one hand, her greatest outburst of self-assertion – 'I want to tell you [Paul] something ... I want to tell you all' (ch. 41) – arises from erotic jealousy and wins her a proposal of marriage. On the other hand, her perverse silences reflect a highly developed instinct to protect the independence and power that she has achieved outside of erotic fulfilment, a power that continues to sustain her after Paul's death. Before this occurs, however, she makes good use of her own and her reader's accumulated strength to support her during the climactic, visionary night in the park when she believes she has lost Paul. Drugged and again alone, she repeatedly calls upon the reader during this scene to share her perception of what she terms the 'TRUTH'. Employing the words 'we' and 'us' in her appeals (ch. 39), she identifies her readers completely with her own perspective and includes them in a deliberate but psychologically necessary misreading of the scene.

At the end of her narrative, when Lucy asks the reader to 'scout the paradox' of her three happiest years, she appeals for the last time to the community she herself has created to grant credence to the highly unconventional conclusion of her tale. She has by this time given us ample warning that 'endings' for women are problematic, and traditional plots no help in assessing her own experience. She has explicitly shared with the reader her final words on the lives of the two more familiar fictional women after their marriages: Ginevra fails to come to the expected bad end, and, in fact, fails to develop at all; and Polly, she cannot help admitting to the reader, however blessed in the resolution of her tale, bears a distinct resemblance to a pampered and adoring spaniel (chs 40, 36).[17] Equally unexpected, perhaps, Lucy's life does not end with Paul's; the observant reader will have noted that the school clearly continues to prosper and that Lucy, by the time she begins her narrative, knows the West End of London as well as her beloved City (ch. 6). Rewriting the traditional novel to illustrate the limited plots available to women in literature, as in life, she has survived the destruction of the romantic fantasy and grown into another reality.

The path, however, to a maturity that is intellectually and financially fulfilling, and I would argue existentially fulfilling as well, involves more than just the telling of the tale; ultimately, Lucy's development resides in the mediation of the reader who grants her the recognition and the reality of her perceptions lacking in the external world. As readers ourselves, to the extent that we can enter into and accept Lucy's cryptic conclusion, we will join 'in friendly company' with the '[p]ilgrims and brother mourners' (ch. 38) who acknowledge pain and hear, as Miss Marchmont did, the unspoken word of encouragement. Otherwise, we remain among those readers whose sunny imaginations still demand conventional endings, and who cannot conceive, as Lucy herself does, that while life for someone in her position is hard, in the reflections provided by the reader she has gained the power to grow and to speak, and with it the power to endure.

From *The Voyage In: Fictions in Female Development*, ed. E. Abel, M. Hirsch and E. Langland (Hanover, 1983), pp. 90–111.

NOTES

[Brenda Silver's essay first appeared in a collection of essays which undertook a feminist revision of the genre of the *Bildungsroman*. The collection, *The Voyage In*, aimed to expose the gender bias inherent in traditional definitions and discussions of the novel of development and to identify distinctively female versions of the *Bildungsroman*. In contending that Lucy is a 'self-consciously reliable' narrator, Brenda Silver's argument runs counter to the common assumptions about Lucy's unreliability. Silver's thesis is based on a close analysis of the relationship that Lucy as narrator constructs through dialogue with the reader – an analysis which, in positing a creative interchange between reader and text, provides an example of 'reader-response' criticism. Ed.]

1. Charlotte Brontë, *Villette* (New York, 1972), ch. 27; all subsequent references are to this edition. Earlier versions of this paper were presented to the Pacific Coast Conference on British Studies and the University Seminary for Feminist Inquiry at Dartmouth College. I am grateful to the members of the University Seminar and to Marianne Hirsch, Paula Mayhew and Thomas Vargish for extremely useful criticism and suggestions.

2. The wording here reflects that in Wolfgang Iser's *The Implied Reader* (Baltimore, 1974), pp. 274–94, although the idea is common to reader-response criticism. For a collection of the classic essays in the field, see *Reader-Response Criticism: From Formalism to Post-Structuralism*, ed. Jane P. Tompkins (Baltimore, 1980); for more recent speculations, see *The Reader in the Text: Essays on Audience and Interpretation*, ed. Susan R. Soleiman and Inge Crossman (Princeton, 1980).

3. Helene Moglen, *Charlotte Brontë: The Self Conceived* (New York, 1978), pp. 196, 199. [An extract from Moglen is reprinted above – see p. 16 Ed.]

4. Mary Jacobus, 'The Buried Letter: Feminism and Romanticism in *Villette*', in *Women Writing and Writing about Women*, ed. Mary Jacobus (London, 1979), p. 43. [Reprinted in this volume – see p. 121 Ed.]

5. Sandra M. Gilbert and Susan Gubar, *The Madwoman in the Attic: The Woman Writer and the Nineteenth-Century Literary Imagination* (New Haven, 1979), pp. 418–19. [An extract from Gilbert and Gubar is reprinted above – see p. 42 Ed.]

6. Tony Tanner shares this reading of the narrative. Lucy, he writes, 'finds

herself in "bad" narrative in which she has effectively to create, or put together, her own ontology and value-system' ('Introduction', in Charlotte Brontë, *Villette* [New York, 1979], p. 49). [An extract from Tanner is reprinted above – see p. 58. Ed.]

7. Nancy Miller, 'Emphasis Added', *PMLA*, 96:1 (January 1981), 36–48.

8. One needs only recall Brontë's bitter comment in her explanation of why she and her sisters chose gender-ambiguous pseudonyms – 'without at that time suspecting that our mode of writing and thinking was not what is called "feminine"' – to measure the effect of criticism such as that in *The Christian Remembrancer* – 'A book more unfeminine, both in its excellences and defects, it would be hard to find in the annals of female authorship' – and that of Elizabeth Rigby in the *Quarterly*: '. . . If we ascribe the book to a woman at all, we have no alternative but to ascribe it to one who has, for some sufficient reason, long forfeited the society of her own sex'. (Charlotte Brontë's comment appears in the 'Biographical Notice' to the 1850 edition of *Wuthering Heights* and *Agnes Grey*, quoted in Inga-Stina Ewbank, *Their Proper Sphere* [Cambridge, Mass., 1968], p. 1; the reviews of *Jane Eyre* are quoted and discussed in Ewbank, pp. 43–6, and in Margot Peters, *Unquiet Soul: A Biography of Charlotte Brontë* [New York, 1976], pp. 237–8.) Brontë was correct, moreover, to anticipate a similar response to *Villette*: Matthew Arnold, for example, found it 'disagreeable. . . . because the writer's mind contains nothing but hunger, rebellion, and rage', and Thackeray criticised it as 'rather vulgar – I don't make my *good women* ready to fall in love with two men at once' (quoted in Peters, p. 429). The most vicious attack, however, was Anne Mozley's anonymous review in *The Christian Remembrancer*. Although granting that the author of *Villette* had 'gained both in amiability and propriety since she first presented herself in the world – soured, coarse and grumbling; an alien, it might seem, from society, and amenable to none of its laws', her final judgement is severe. Brontë's 'impersonations' are branded as 'self-reliant' and 'contemptuous of prescriptive decorum', and of Lucy she writes: 'We will sympathise with Lucy Snowe as being fatherless and penniless . . . but we cannot offer even the affections of our fancy (the right and due of every legitimate heroine) to her unscrupulous and self-dependent intellect.' Responding to this attack in a letter to the editor of the journal, Brontë consistently refers to the reviewer as 'he'. (The extracts of Mozley's review [June 1853] and Brontë's response [July 1853] appear in T. J. Wise and J. A. Symington (eds), *The Brontës: Their Lives, Friendships and Correspondence* [Oxford, 1932], vol. 4, pp. 78–9, and in Peters, *Unquiet Soul*, p. 428.)

For a discussion of nineteenth-century criticism of women's fiction, including Brontë's, see Elaine Showalter's chapter 'The Double Critical Standard', in *A Literature of Their Own: British Women Novelists from Brontë to Lessing* (Princeton, 1977).

9. For another understanding of the 'oddly assorted female Powers who people the novel's cosmos', see Nina Auerbach's chapter on *Villette* in *Communities of Women* (Cambridge, Mass., 1978), p. 110.

10. Kate Millet, *Sexual Politics* (New York, 1971), p. 193. [See p. 32 above. Ed.]

11. Speaking of Mrs Bretton's 'patronage' of her, Lucy remarks, 'it was not founded on conventional grounds of superior wealth or station (in the last particular there had never been any inequality; her degree was mine)' (ch. 16). I stress this point as a corrective to Terry Eagleton's analysis of Lucy's class anger and its effect on her psychological life, an analysis which overlooks the role of gender in connection with class (*Myths of Power: A Marxist Study of the Brontës* [New York, 1975]). [An extract from Eagleton is reprinted below – see p. 107. Ed.]

12. M. Jeanne Peterson, 'The Victorian Governess: Status Incongruence in Family and Society', in *Suffer and Be Still: Women in the Victorian Age*, ed. Martha Vicinus (Bloomington, 1973), p. 16.

13. Helene Moglen interprets this linguistic pattern as part of Lucy's anaesthetised reaction to the guilt of being a survivor, a way of not having to participate in life, and labels it neurotic (see, for example, pp. 196, 203, in *The Self Conceived* [New York, 1978]). Terry Eagleton, looking at this same language, reads it as part of Lucy's (and Jane Eyre's) need to see herself as a 'meek, unworldly victim unable to act purposively' in order not to be accused of self-interested enterprise and the desire for social advancement (*Myths of Power* [New York, 1975], pp. 62–3). The truth is, however, that no matter how strong Lucy's energy and will, she would not have acquired her own school nearly as soon without Paul's gift, nor could she have expanded it as rapidly without Miss Marchmont's legacy. These are economic realities.

14. Nancy Miller is here quoting from Barbara Bellow Watson, 'On Power and the Literary Text', *Signs*, I (1975) 113.

15. Mary Jacobus argues that 'The novel's real oddity lies in perversely withholding its true subject, Lucy Snowe, by an act of repression which mimics hers', and that 'Lucy's invisibility is a calculated deception – a blank screen on which others project their view of her' ('The Buried Letter' in *Women Writing and Writing about Women*, ed. Mary Jacobus [London, 1979], pp. 43, 44). The nun, on the other hand, forces the reader to experience the 'uncanny' aspect of Lucy's narrative and becomes the true mirror of the hidden self (p. 52). I would argue that rather than perversely withholding its true subject, Lucy's narrative deliberately illustrates why the true subject is invisible to those with conventional social and fictional expectations. Lucy's true fiction is there from the beginning, created in part through the dialogue with the reader.

16. See, for example, the four addresses to the reader in ch. 18, 'We Quarrel'.

17. Observations about Ginevra and Polly continue to be addressed directly
    to the reader throughout the narrative, for here Lucy's perceptions do
    perhaps differ most radically from those of a society that might well find
    her merely jealous. Toward Ginevra she is continually sarcastic, but her
    attitude toward Polly is more complex. Ultimately, however, she
    underlines the conventional quality in Polly which leads the younger
    woman to respond to Lucy's understanding that 'solitude is sadness' but
    not death. '"Lucy, I wonder if anybody will ever comprehend you
    altogether"' (ch. 37).

7

Myths of Power in 'Villette'

TERRY EAGLETON

When Jane Eyre turns on Mrs Reed, hotly accusing her of cruelty and neglect, she is quick to point out to the reader that her outburst is in no sense consciously calculated:

> 'What would uncle Reed say to you, if he were alive?' was my scarcely voluntary demand. I say scarcely voluntary, for it seemed as if my tongue pronounced words without my will consenting to their utterance: something spoke out of me over which I had no control.[1]

The novel needs to stress the 'scarcely voluntary' nature of Jane's denunciation, for to do otherwise would risk seriously damaging our image of her. Jane's comment is, indeed, dexterously cutting and well placed, accurately launched at her guardian's most vulnerable spot; and it is to avoid any suggestion of vindictiveness (not least on the part of a child) that the spontaneity of the remark is underlined. It is not the only place in *Jane Eyre* where the novelist resorts to such a device. A similar gambit is adopted when Jane, about to leave Lowood school, is pondering her future career:

> A kind fairy, in my absence, had surely dropped the required suggestion on my pillow; for as I lay down it came quietly and naturally to my mind: – 'Those who want situations advertise; you must advertise in the —*shire Herald.*'
> 'How? I know nothing about advertising.'
> Replies rose smooth and prompt now: –
> 'You must enclose the advertisement and the money to pay for it under a cover directed to the Editor of the *Herald*; you must put it, at the first opportunity you have, into the post at Lowton; answers must

be addressed to J. E. at the post-office there; you can go and inquire in about a week after you send your letter, if any are come, and act accordingly.'[2]

This brisk, unwittingly comic interior dialogue takes place between two facets of Jane: the meek, unworldly victim unable to act purposively, and the enterprising activist with an efficient knowledge of the measures essential for social advancement. That second Jane is repressed, depersonalised to a subconscious voice, sharply distinguished from the 'real' Jane who lacks the dynamism to succeed. The effect, then, is to show Jane moving eagerly forward without the objectionable implication that she is egoistically drafting her future. By the clumsy device of the divided self, Jane is able to make progress without detriment to her innocent passivity. Her return to Rochester is similarly engineered:

> I saw nothing, but I heard a voice somewhere cry –
> 'Jane! Jane! Jane!' nothing more.
> 'O God! what is it?' I gasped.
> I might have said, 'Where is it?' for it did not seem in the room – nor in the house – nor in the garden; it did not come out of the air – nor from under the earth – nor from overhead. I had heard it – where, or whence, for ever impossible to know! And it was the voice of a human being – a known, loved, well-remembered voice – that of Edward Fairfax Rochester; and it spoke in pain and woe wildly, eerily, urgently.[3]

Lucy Snowe, the heroine of *Villette*, is also prompted to significant decisions by an involuntary power. It inspires her movement from the Midlands to London:

> A bold thought was sent to my mind; my mind was made strong to receive it.
> 'Leave this wilderness,' it was said to me, 'and go out hence.'
> 'Where?' was the query.
> I had not very far to look; gazing from this country parish in that flat, rich middle of England – I mentally saw within reach what I had never yet beheld with my bodily eyes: I saw London.[4]

The same inner voice guides her to Villette and, having got her there, proves omniscient enough to know the precise residence she must visit: 'About a hundred thoughts volleyed through my mind in a moment. Yet I planned nothing, and considered nothing: I had not time. Providence said, 'Stop here; this is *your* inn.' Fate took me in her strong hand; mastered my will; directed my actions; I rang the door-bell.'[5]

This miraculous propulsion from point to point, in a process which will turn out to be one of social advancement, is enough to absolve Lucy from a charge of self-interested calculation; and it is an essential stratagem for resolving the Jane-like contradiction in her character. Lucy is presented to begin with as a spectatorial outsider; like Jane she is an alien in another's home, able to pride herself only on a coolly analytic brand of observation. 'I, Lucy Snowe, was calm',[6] she declares, when neutrally recounting Polly Home's anguish at the departure of her father from the Bretton household. Yet her attitude towards the enigmatic Polly is intensely ambiguous: her heavily prosaic, taciturnly critical, Nelly Dean-like grimness with the girl (she is full of 'maxims of philosophy' with which to fend off Polly's tantalising blend of pertness and plangency) is so clearly self-defensive that it succeeds only in drawing attention to the firmly repressed fascination she feels for her more privileged, more emotionally vulnerable but also oddly opaque and self-possessed companion:

> I, Lucy Snowe, plead guiltless of that curse, an overheated and discursive imagination; but whenever, opening a room-door, I found her seated in a corner alone, her head in her pigmy hand, that room seemed to me not inhabited, but haunted.[7]

Lucy's attitude to Polly is, in fact, a subconscious tactical conversion of suppressed jealousy to mature condescension; a sort of malice is rationalised as a briskly commonsensical taking in hand. Polly is a 'little creature': she compares herself indirectly to a cat, as Ginevra Fanshawe is later compared spitefully to a mouse. She is spoilt, perverse but piquant, and so both resented and grudgingly admired. The capriciousness in her which attracts Graham Bretton suggests aspects of Lucy's own concealed emotional life; and in that sense Lucy's tight-lipped treatment of the girl signifies the erection of a blandly rational barrier against her own coldly unacknowledged impulses. Lucy projects herself into Polly and then coolly dissociates herself from that self-image, as indeed does Polly herself in public: 'Whilst lavishing her eccentricities regardlessly before me ... she never showed my godmother one glimpse of her inner self: for her, she was nothing but a docile, somewhat quaint little maiden.'[8]

As a small but socially fortunate child, then, Polly is irritatingly imperious but also touchingly helpless; and in this sense she reflects a contradiction inherent in Lucy herself. Lucy, too, is both vulnerable and strenuously self-reliant, and the novel has to work hard to preserve a balance between the two. She wants a sheltered life in the Bretton household, even if this means sacrificing 'the charm of variety . . . the excitement of incident';[9] she sees herself as 'prosaic', 'Tame and still by habit, disciplined by destiny',[10] and feels the need of external stimulus to goad her into life:

> It seemed I must be stimulated into action. I must be goaded, driven, stung, forced to energy. . . . I had wanted to compromise with Fate: to escape occasional great agonies by submitting to a whole life of privation and small pains. Fate would not so be pacified; nor would Providence sanction this shrinking sloth and cowardly indolence.[11]

Is being forced into the wider world merely a harsh fate, inferior to remaining obscurely cloistered, or is that shy withdrawal from society really 'shrinking sloth and cowardly indolence', and worldly progress therefore a positive good? Lucy herself is significantly unsure, finding herself friendless in London but also enthralled by the turmoil of the City: ' "How is this?" said I. "Methinks I am animated and alert, instead of being depressed and apprehensive?" '[12] Miserable though she is on her first lonely night in London, she has no wish to retract the step she has taken: 'A strong, vague persuasion that it was better to go forward than backward, and that I *could* go forward – that a way, however narrow and difficult, would in time open – predominated over other feelings. . . .'[13] Despite her insecurity, she has a proper scorn for those bemused foreigners who marvel at the intrepidity of English girls travelling alone.

As both enterprising individualist and helpless victim, Lucy is caught in an interior conflict similar to Jane's. The trajectory of both girls' careers is much the same: propelled from an initial settlement into the promise and terror of independence, both need to swallow back treacherous fantasies in the drive to carve a worldly niche. Yet Lucy is closer to William Crimsworth in her more articulate social ambition: 'unadventurous' though she declares herself, she also confesses contradictorily that her 'mind was a good deal bent on success'.[14] Passivity and self-denial bring social benefits in all of Charlotte's novels, as Lucy discovers in a minor way when she first encounters snobbish servants in a London inn: 'Maintaining a very quiet manner towards this arrogant little maid, and subsequently observing the same towards the parsonic-looking, black-coated, white-neckclothed waiter, I got civility from them ere long.'[15] But whereas in *Jane Eyre* this truth remains secretively implicit, the unilluminated underside of the novel, Lucy Snowe is allowed to formulate it into an explicit project for self-advancement: 'Courage, Lucy Snowe! With self-denial and economy now, and steady exertion by-and-by, an object in life need not fail you.'[16]

Lucy's internal contradictions can be charted most clearly in her thoroughly ambiguous attitude towards her employer, Madame Beck. Madame Beck is a spying, scheming little bourgeoise who privately examines the contents of Lucy's luggage when she first arrives; but Lucy is notably generous in her excusal of this action. ('Her duty done – I felt that in her eyes this business was a duty – she rose, noiselessly as a shadow. . . .')[17] The text of the novel is jumpily unpredictable in its variations of hostility and approbation: Madame Beck's watchwords are 'Surveillance, espionage',[18] yet she knows what honesty is – 'that is, when it did not intrude its clumsy scruples in the way of her will and interest'.[19] She seems to know that keeping girls in restraint and blind ignorance is not the best way to educate them, and we are about to applaud her liberalism when we learn her opinion that 'ruinous consequences would ensue if any other method were tried with continental children'.[20] Her system is 'easy, liberal, salutary, and rational',[21] yet we hear later that she rears minds in Romish slavery; she is 'Wise, firm, faithless, secret, crafty',[22] but is judged by Lucy to be 'a very great and a very capable woman'[23] – until, that is, she is finally exposed as a thorough villain. If the reader is at a loss to know what to make of Madame Beck, the novel itself seems equally mystified.

That bemusement has its root in Lucy's own vacillating response to her superior – vacillating because Madame Beck is at once her oppressor and an image of the icy rational power she herself wants to possess. Her spying is naturally resented, but it also stirs Lucy's Romantic sensibilities: Madame Beck's noiseless gliding about the school reminds us of the equally elusive 'ghost', to whom Lucy reacts with a similar compound of commonsensical scorn and covert fascination. Like her school, Madame Beck is a curious mixture of rational benevolence and oppressive restraint; her stoical self-composure appeals to Lucy's own dourly rationalist streak, but its tantalising opacity is also imaginatively seductive.

Madame Beck's frigid calm, then, is both criticised and approved; and indeed the novel's categorial structure is built chiefly around a set of oppositions between calm and storm, calculative rationalism and Romantic impulse, self-possession and emotional self-exposure.

Lucy lives at the focal point of these tensions, and their resolution is to be found in the figure of her fiery little lover, Paul Emanuel. ('Little' is significant: Paul is domineering but, like Hunsden, physically slight, as Madame Beck, conversely, appears occasionally like a man.) Fiery though he is, Paul is also puritanically austere, and so provides Lucy with precisely the right amalgam of passion and censoriousness. He is, in fact, a kind of Hunsden, scoffing but covertly a soul-mate, caustic but secretly charitable. Like Madame Beck he is a sly intriguer, but unlike her he is turbulent, impetuous and hair-raisingly ferocious into the bargain.

Rumour has it that Paul was educated by Jesuits, and Jesuits, as the fearful epitome of Roman Catholicism for Charlotte, are associated at once with worldly deviousness and ascetic absolutism, manipulative cunning and cloak-and-dagger Romance. Since the quarrel between worldly and ascetic forms of religion is an important one in Charlotte's fiction, not least in its treatment of Evangelicalism, it is worth adding a digressive note on it here. In so far as Evangelicalism sets out to crush the Romantic spirit, it is a tangible symbol of social violence and must be resisted. Jane Eyre rebels against Brocklehurst's cruel cant and Rivers's deathly Calvinism; she also scorns Eliza Reed's decision to enter a Roman Catholic convent, viewing this as a falsely ascetic withdrawal from the world. But she is at the same time 'Quakerish' herself, grimly disapproving of worldly libertinism; and in this sense she is torn between respect for and instinctive distrust of stringent religious discipline, caught between pious submission and defiant rebellion. Charlotte Brontë's attitudes to Evangelicalism are, in short, thoroughly ambiguous, as is obvious enough if the detestable Brocklehurst is placed in the balance against the treatment of spoilt children in the novels, where evangelical attitudes to childhood strongly emerge. The theme of pampered, perverse children crops up in almost all the Brontës' novels, and the evangelical responses involved with it are clearly, in part, class-responses: exasperated reactions to the indolent offspring of the rich, as in Anne Brontë's talk of the need to crush vicious tendencies in the bud in the Bloomfield family scenes of *Agnes Grey*. It is an evangelical impulse to avoid 'cowardly indolence' and sally out instead to put one's soul to the test which motivates Lucy's journey to Villette; it is a similar impulse which brings Caroline Helstone to reject as false, Romish superstition the idea that virtue lies in self-abnegation, and decide instead to become a governess. What Hunsden sees as attractive 'spirit' in Crimsworth's son Victor, Crimsworth himself interprets as 'the leaven of the offending Adam',[24] and considers that it should be, if not whipped out of him, at least soundly disciplined.

Evangelical discipline, then, is hateful in its sour oppressiveness but useful in curbing the libertine, over-assertive self. It is to be rejected in so far as, like Rivers's Calvinism, it turns one away from the world, but welcomed as a spur to worldly effort and achievement. At the same time, religion can clearly be *too* worldly; and this is true in *Villette* of Roman Catholicism, whose clergy are condemned as 'mitred aspirants for this world's kingdoms'.[25] On the other hand, the Roman Church is despised with healthy, rational, Protestant contempt for its lurid superstition and primitive otherworldliness; and in this ambivalence it becomes a microcosm of the 'foreign' in general. Belgium in *Villette* is portrayed as a flat, drab expanse peopled by dreary, lumpish bourgeois, a mundane and materialist enclave; but it is also a land of mystery and imbroglio, of plotting, drugging and haunting. The 'foreign' in Charlotte's fiction offers an imaginative adventure absent at home: its very alienness converts it to a blank surface on to which private fantasies may be feverishly projected. Yet since that alienness is entwined with spying and oppression, it intensifies the claustrophobic home environment as well as providing an escape from it.

What Paul Emanuel represents, in effect, is an agreeable combination of Hunsden and Frances Henri, as his lecture in the *Tribune* reveals:

> Who would have thought the flat and fat soil of Labassecour could yield political convictions and national feelings, such as were now strongly expressed? Of the bearing of his opinions I need here give no special indication: yet it may be permitted me to say I believed the little man not more earnest than right in what he said: with all his fire he was severe and sensible; he trampled Utopian theories under his heels; he rejected wild dreams with scorn; – but, when he looked in the face of tyranny – oh, then there opened a light in his eye worth seeing; and when he spoke of injustice, his voice gave no uncertain sound, but reminded me rather of the band-trumpet, ringing at twilight from the park.[26]

Paul unites a 'sensible' anti-radicalism with fiery reformist zeal, Protestant rationalism with Catholic spirit; if he shares Frances Henri's conservative patriotism, he also has something of Hunsden's scorching contempt for political reaction. He is a man 'always somewhat shy at meeting the advances of the wealthy'[27] and, like Lucy, has known poverty, having starved for a year in a Rome garret.

Because he is passionate himself, he alone can appreciate the true Lucy behind the protective facade; he sees shrewdly that her calm conceals a storm like his, and believes consequently in chastising her: 'You want so much checking, regulating, and keeping down.'[28] Lucy finds the discipline energising, and is flattered that one man at least has intuited her hidden imaginative depths in a society which obtusely takes her skilfully contrived sangfroid at face-value. Paul's censoriousness, then, is not merely that of a hard-headed English Protestant grimly extirpating the sin of fancy, although Lucy welcomes it as a curb to her guilty imaginings; it also imputes to her a vivacity and inner complexity to which others are dully insensitive, and so reveals Paul's own attractive subtlety of perception. In so far as it is part of Paul's Jesuitism, it is at least as impressive a form of despotism as Madame Beck's crafty schemings. Both Roman Catholicism and Protestantism, in fact combine rigorous self-discipline with imaginative intensity: Lucy speaks of Methodist and Papist as equally fantastical, and indeed the Romish tract which Paul gives her reminds her of Wesleyan pamphlets read in childhood.

Paul tells Lucy at one point that she needs 'watching, and watching over',[29] and that verbal conjunction says much about their relationship. Being watched is objectionable, but in so far as it involves being watched over − cared for − it is clearly desirable. To be critically scrutinised by another at least implies a negative form of interest on his part, perhaps the most you can hope for in a hostile, treacherous society. Paul's constant secret surveillance of all the school's inmates from his lattice-window links him closely to the oppressive world of Villette but also lends him a seductive air of divinity, raises him above routine pettiness and plotting. Even so, Lucy does not allow herself to be seduced without a struggle. When she finds Paul 'sullying the shield of Britannia, and dabbling the union-jack in the mud' in the course of a particularly vitriolic harangue to his students, she is quickly stung to chauvinist contempt for 'these clowns of Labassecour', striking her desk with a resounding cry of 'Vive l'Angleterre, l'Histoire et les Héros!'[30] It is Frances and Hunsden once more, but the conflict is this time more complex. For whereas Frances is simply a conservative patriot, Lucy is also a latent rebel; and it is the latency of that rebelliousness which constitutes one of the most interesting features of *Villette*. It emerges most obviously in her ambiguous attitude towards the Bretton family, and especially towards the alluring young John. The Brettons have the genuine sangfroid of which Lucy's coolness is a contrived, self-protective parody; and as such they win from her a kind of admiring envy. She feels unable to recount her harrowing experiences to Mrs Bretton because of the difference of circumstance between them:

> The difference between her and me might be figured by that between the stately ship cruising safe on smooth seas, with its full complement of crew, a captain gay and brave, and venturous and provident; and the life-boat, which most days of the year lies dry and solitary in an old, dark boat-house, only putting to sea when the billows run high in rough weather, when cloud encounters water, when danger and death divide between them the rule of the great deep.[31]

The contrast goes formally in Mrs Bretton's favour: respectable women of her kind are not to be affronted by sordid tales of mental anguish. She is, Lucy comments elsewhere, 'an English middle-class gentlewoman'[32] – 'English' making the difference, since the Belgian burghers are universally despised. Yet the novel has constantly to repress under this 'official' attitude a flickering resentment of that English bourgeois blandness epitomised by the Brettons and gratifyingly absent in Paul.

Lucy's view of John Bretton, for example, grows stealthily more critical as the novel develops, without ever declaring itself directly. The play staged at the school under Paul's direction is a case in point. Lucy plays a foppish male wooer of Ginevra Fanshawe, the coquette with whom John is in love; and the fact that John is in the audience spurs her on to 'woo' Ginevra from him. She does this because she herself loves John and wants to separate him from Ginevra; but since she is also symbolically competing with Bretton, the act expresses at the same time a certain oblique antagonism to him. Her 'wooing' of Ginevra is equally double-edged: it releases her hostility to the girl, since its aim is to divorce her from Bretton, but also signifies a grudging admiration for Ginevra's success and an impulse to identify with her. (Ginevra, she discovers later, is gradually becoming for her a kind of heroine, even though she sees this to be an illusion; despite her 'plain prose knowledge' of the empty-headed Society flirt, 'a kind of reflected glow began to settle on her idea'.)[33] Since Lucy loves the man who loves Ginevra, there is a sense in which she loves Ginevra too; and since Ginevra treats Lucy in the play as a substitute John, Lucy is out to attract her. In so far as Lucy's behaviour suggests a desire to oust Ginevra from John's affections but also to unlodge John from Ginevra's, it reveals her ambiguous approval and resentment of those more successful than herself. It implies a loving concern for Bretton and a competitive jealousy of him, a fascination for Ginevra and a desire to injure her. Lucy has commented sharply in an early aside that she thought the young John thoroughly spoilt; and she is certainly irritated later by the absurdity of his love for Ginevra. She is also ready to admit that he is cruelly vain, lacks sympathetic warmth and is in some ways emotionally shallow; but at the same time his very incapacity for emotional turbulence contrasts favourably with Paul's choler. John offers rest and refuge; but the novel, while like all Charlotte's work deeply committed to a dream of placid self-fulfilment, also has a needling animus against it – the animus of the socially inferior whose lot is to suffer distraction and despair. John is 'a cheerful fellow by nature',[34] and soon recovers from Ginevra's rejection of him; but this resilience, while in a sense applauded, also reveals that lack of complex emotional depth which leads him to see Lucy herself superficially:

> 'I wish I could tell [Polly] all I recall; or rather, I wish some one, *you* for instance, would go behind and whisper it all in her ear, and I could have the delight – here, as I sit – of watching her look under the intelligence. Could you manage that, think you, Lucy, and make me ever grateful?'
> 'Could I manage to make you ever grateful?' said I. 'No, *I could not.*' And I felt my fingers work and my hands interlock: I felt, too, an inward courage, warm and resistant. In this matter I was not disposed to gratify Dr John: not at all. With now welcome force, I realized his entire misapprehension of my character and nature. He wanted always to give me a role not mine. Nature and I opposed him. He did not at all guess what I felt: he did not read my eyes, or face, or gestures; though, I doubt not, all spoke. Leaning towards me coaxingly, he said softly, '*Do* content me, Lucy'.[35]

The passage teeters on the edge of a sardonic poke at John's sentimental egoism, but just manages to repress its tartness. A page later, we are back to eulogising the dashing young doctor: 'Dr John, throughout his whole life, was a man of luck – a man of success. And why? Because he had the eye to see his opportunity, the heart to prompt to well-timed action, the nerve to consummate a perfect work. . . .'[36] This, indeed, is the final, 'official' verdict; the novel's subcurrent of resentment, stemmed by the overriding need to celebrate bourgeois security, is forbidden to break disruptively through the book's surface. Lucy's bitterness at John's breezy treatment of her is clearly a class-issue – 'Had Lucy been intrinsically the same, but possessing the additional advantages of wealth and station, would your manner to her, your value for her, have been quite what they actually were?'[37] – but it is a bitterness prudently quelled. The smooth, stately life-style of a Mrs Bretton, subconscious irritant though it may be to the poor and dispossessed, symbolises none the less a point of aspiration and stability which must at all costs be preserved.

Even so, the novel's option to unite Lucy to Paul rather than John speaks eloquently enough. (Lucy loses nothing socially by this move, of course, since Paul is of a wealthy background and John is not of aristocratic stock.) The opposition between the two men is one between convention and eccentricity, domesticity and solitariness, the English and the alien, gentility and passion; but those tensions are contained and negotiated by the book's refusal to allow a Rochester–Rivers kind of confrontation between them. *Villette* is in some ways a more tragic work than *Jane Eyre*, but it is also more accommodating, more concerned to muffle direct antagonism. Like Jane, Lucy lives as a child in someone else's household, but unlike Jane she is 'a good deal taken notice of';[38] and since she is therefore less of an exile she is less ready to rebel. The world is to be temporised with rather than subversively challenged; Lucy maintains, against Ginevra Fanshawe's jejune snobbery, that pedigree and social position are of minor importance, but 'The world, I soon learned, held a different estimate: and I make no doubt, the world is very right in its view, yet believe also that I am not quite wrong in mine.'[39] That 'not quite wrong' proves ominous: as Lucy goes on to tease out the contradiction, the balance tips quietly on the side of the world.

The tensions are also contained by the fact that Paul Emanuel, like Shirley and unlike Hunsden, is a rebel more in style than substance. He may be tempestuously individualist, but it is he who is morally outraged to find Lucy viewing a nude portrait in a local art-gallery, and she who is thereby cast into the role of quirkily independent Englishwoman. Lucy's response to the portrait is significant: it embodies a crude, overblown naturalism, and her distaste for it suggests a cultural superiority to the prosaic Belgians at the same time as it manifests a brusquely commonsensical English philistinism. There is a similar ambivalence in her reaction to the theatrical performance to which Bretton takes her: she finds it at once stupendous and sordid. ('It was a marvellous sight: a mighty revelation. It was a spectacle low, horrible, immoral.'[40]) Englishpuritan and European-Romantic jostle each other uneasily; indeed, one of their rare points of fusion in the novel is in the figure of Polly's father, Mr Home, who is part Scots and part French aristocrat, 'at once proud-looking and homely-looking',[41] combining Gallic grace with Scots ruggedness. In a telling irony, one of the few admirable European aristocrats in the book (French, significantly, rather than lumpishly Belgian) turns out to be partly Scots.

Moreover, Paul Emanuel does finally offer Lucy, as Rochester ultimately offers Jane, both emotional fulfilment *and* a sheltered refuge. He sets her up in business as a private teacher, providing her with a well-appointed residence. The ambiguity of the novel's ending – is Paul drowned or not? – is then appropriate to the book's continually double-edged attitude to the question of secure settlement. Even on the brink of disaster, happiness is not allowed to be wholly snatched away; it survives as an ideal possibility which might validate the suffering channelled into its achievement. Yet suffering, on the other hand, is too palpable to be merely swallowed up into felicity; and so the conclusion remains calculatedly unresolved, underlining the delights of domestic settlement at the same time as it protests against the bland unreality of such an ending, witnessing to the truth of an emotional agony which cannot be simply wished away. In the end, the novel is unable to opt for either possibility: it cannot betray its sense of the reality of failure, but swerves nervously away from the corollary that this might imply – that worldly achievement may be empty and invalid. In the end, *Villette* has neither the courage to be tragic nor to be comic; like all of Charlotte's novels, although in its conclusion more obviously than any, it is a kind of middle-ground, a half-measure.

From Terry Eagleton, *Myths of Power: A Marxist Study of the Brontës* (London, 1975), pp. 61–73.

NOTES

[Terry Eagleton's essay first appeared as the fourth chapter of his book on the Brontës. Eagleton's study anticipated later poststructuralist readings in its focus on the 'ambiguous' and 'internally divided' nature of Charlotte Brontë's work. However, while the poststructuralist might regard this division as inherent in the nature of language, Eagleton, as a Marxist, sees the division as the result of an ideological tension between rebellion and conformity and he argues that such division can be read as 'a fictionally transformed version of the tensions and alliances between the two social classes which dominated the Brontës' world: the industrial bourgeoisie, and the landed gentry or aristocracy' (p. 4). Eagleton's book provided the first extended Marxist analysis of the work of the Brontës. The influence of Marxist criticism since then has been most evident in the work of feminist critics like Penny Boumelha, who have combined the analysis of gender with that of class (see, for example, Penny Boumelha, *Charlotte Brontë* [Hemel Hempstead, 1990]).Ed.]

1. Charlotte Brontë, *Jane Eyre*, ed. Mrs H. Ward and C. K. Shorter (London, 1899–1900), ch. 4, p. 26.

2. Ibid., ch. 10, p. 100.

3. Ibid., ch. 35, p. 513.

4. Charlotte Brontë, *Villette*, ed. Mrs H. Ward and C. K. Shorter (London, 1899–1900), ch. 5, p. 47.

5. Ibid., ch. 7, pp. 71–2.

6. Ibid., ch. 3, p. 21.

7. Ibid., ch. 2, p. 9.

8. Ibid., ch. 3, p. 33.

9. Ibid., ch. 1, p. 2.

10. Ibid., ch. 4, p. 39.

11. Ibid., ch. 4, pp. 39–40.

12. Ibid., ch. 6, p. 56.

13. Ibid., ch. 5, p. 51.

14. Ibid., ch. 9, p. 94.

15. Ibid., ch. 5, p. 50.

16. Ibid., ch. 31, p. 431.

17. Ibid., ch. 8, p. 78.

18. Ibid., ch. 8, p. 82.

19. Ibid., ch. 8, p. 82.

20. Ibid., ch. 8, p. 82.

21. Ibid., ch. 8, p. 83.

22. Ibid., ch. 8, p. 84.

23. Ibid., ch. 8, p. 84.

24. Charlotte Brontë, *The Professor*, ed. Mrs H. Ward and C. K. Shorter (London, 1899–1900), ch. 25, p. 271.

25. Charlotte Brontë, *Villette* (London, 1899–1900), ch. 36, p. 504.
26. Ibid., ch. 27, p. 371.
27. Ibid., ch. 27, p. 372.
28. Ibid., ch. 31, p. 433.
29. Ibid., ch. 31, p. 433.
30. Ibid., ch. 29, p. 406.
31. Ibid., ch. 17, p. 212.
32. Ibid., ch. 20, p. 258.
33. Ibid., ch. 17, p. 226.
34. Ibid., ch. 22, p. 296.
35. Ibid., ch. 27, p. 379.
36. Ibid., ch. 27, p. 380.
37. Ibid., ch. 27, p. 376.
38. Ibid., ch. 1, p. 1.
39. Ibid., ch. 27, p. 369.
40. Ibid., ch. 23, p. 306.
41. Ibid., ch. 2, p. 11.

8

The Buried Letter: Feminism and Romanticism in 'Villette'

MARY JACOBUS

Repression:

> Is this enough? Is it to live? . . . Does virtue lie in abnegation of self? I do not believe it. . . . Each human being has his share of rights. I suspect it would conduce to the happiness and welfare of all, if each knew his allotment, and held to it as tenaciously as the martyr to his creed. Queer thoughts, these, that surge in my mind: are they right thoughts? I am not certain.
>
> *(Shirley* [1849], ch. X)

Caroline Helstone's assertion of the inalienable rights of self, in *Shirley*, I take to be the seed of *Villette* (1853) – a novel in which repression returns vengefully on the heroine in the form of a ghostly nun.[1] But *Villette* is not simply about the perils of repression. It is a text formally fissured by its own repressions; concealing a buried letter. Lucy Snowe writes two letters to Graham Bretton, one 'under the dry, stinting check of Reason', the other 'according to the full, liberal impulse of Feeling' (ch. XXII) – one for his benefit, censored and punishingly rational, the other for hers, an outpouring of her innermost self. The same doubleness informs the novel as a whole, making it secretive, unstable and subversive. The narrative and representational conventions of Victorian realism are constantly threatened by an incompletely repressed Romanticism. Supernatural haunting and satanic revolt, delusion and dream, disrupt a text which can give no formal recognition to either Romantic or Gothic modes. The buried letter of Romanticism becomes the discourse of the Other, as the novel's unconscious – not just Lucy's – struggles for articulation within the confines of mid-nineteenth-century realism. The resulting distortions and mutilations in themselves constitute an aspect of the novel's meaning, like the distortions of a dream-text. But there is more to be found in *Villette* than the incompatibility of realist and Romantic modes. It is haunted by the unacknowledged phantom of feminism, and by the strangeness of fiction itself. Its displacements and substitutions, like its silences and dislocations, are a reminder that fiction is the peculiar reserve both of repression and of the *Unheimliche* – the uncanny which, in Freud's words, 'is in reality nothing new or alien, but something which is familiar and old-established in the mind and which has become alienated from it only through the process of repression'.[2] Lucy's haunted self-estrangement encodes the novel's alienation from its ghostly subtext.

Neurosis and ex-centricity: 'Why is *Villette* disagreeable?' asked Matthew Arnold – 'Because the writer's mind contains nothing but hunger, rebellion and rage, and therefore that is all she can, in fact put into her book.'[3] The same qualities inspire Kate Millett's pole-micising of *Villette* as a radical feminist text ('one long meditation on a prison break').[4] Arnold and Millett are alike in proposing an unmediated relationship between author and work. It is easy to dismiss this collapsing of Charlotte Brontë and her fictional creation, Lucy Snowe; in her letters the novelist writes punitively of her heroine, 'I can hardly express what subtlety of thought made me decide upon giving her a cold name' and 'I am not leniently disposed towards Miss *Frost* . . . I never meant to appoint her lines in pleasant places'.[5] Yet the assumption that autobiographical release fuels the novel is natural enough, and not only because the letters evince the same straining after dissociation as the novel itself. For *Villette*, belonging as it appears to do to the tradition of the *roman personnel* (the lived fiction), invites its readers to make just such a covert identification between Charlotte Brontë and her creation – and then frustrates it. The novel's real oddity lies in perversely withholding its true subject, Lucy Snowe, by an act of repression which mimics hers. Her invisibility is more than evasive; it is devious, duplicitous. Lucy lies to us. Her deliberate ruses, omissions and falsifications break the unwritten contract of first-person narrative (the confidence between reader and 'I') and unsettle our faith in the reliability of the text. 'I,

Lucy Snowe, plead guiltless of that curse, an overheated and discursive imagination' (ch. II), she tells us; but the same sentence goes on to speak of the infant Paulina's incommensurately powerful grief 'haunting' the room – as Lucy herself will later be haunted by the 'discursive' imagination she denies. 'I, Lucy Snowe, was calm,' she insists again, after a heart-rending account of Paulina's parting from her father (disclosing the lie): 'she dropped on her knees at a chair with a cry – "Papa!" It was low and long; a sort of "Why hast thou forsaken me?"' (ch. III). Riven with such contradictions, Lucy's narrative calls itself in question by forcing us to misread it. 'I seemed to hold two lives – the life of thought, and that of reality' (ch. VIII), she tells us later; the hidden life of thought strives ceaselessly to evade her censorship in the very language she uses: that of super-natural haunting and the Christian Passion – the product of an inverted martyrdom in which Lucy renounces her share of rights instead of cleaving to them.

Displacement: at the start of the novel, Lucy observes and narrates another's drama, the diminutive Paulina's. Of her own painful circumstances we learn only that she has been shipwrecked in the metaphoric tempest which recurs at moments of crisis through the novel ('To this hour, when I have the nightmare, it repeats the rush and saltiness of briny waves in my throat, and their icy pressure on my lungs' [ch. IV]). Paulina's grief – that of the abandoned child cast among strangers – has in any case already acted out Lucy's. Asking no pity for herself, Lucy earlier had invoked it for her surrogate: ' "How will she get through this world, or battle with this life? How will she bear the shocks and repulses, the humiliations and desolations. . . ?" ' (ch. III). So, too, Paulina's premature love for the adolescent Graham Bretton is at once a displacement and a pre-figuration of Lucy's future relationship with him; just as, later, Miss Marchmont's state of erotic arrest and confinement are annexed to Lucy herself: 'Two hot, close rooms thus became my world . . . All within me became narrowed to my lot' (ch. IV). As the novel quarries deeper into Lucy's subconscious, the displacement becomes more bizarre. Confined alone at the Rue Fossette during the long vacation, she finds herself looking after a cretin – a creature conjured from nowhere to be her 'strange, deformed companion', an image of deranged self who 'would sit for hours together moping and mowing and distorting her features with indescribable grimaces' (ch. XV). That the heart-sick Miss Marchmont and the untamed cretin, warped in mind and body, are aspects of Lucy's repression (as

Paulina had been an aspect of her loss) hardly needs emphasising. Her regression from child to invalid to cretin parodies and reverses the Romantic quest for self which is the real 'plot' (the conspiracy of silence) of *Villette*. ' "Who *are* you, Miss Snowe?" ', asks Ginevra Fanshawe inquisitively – ' "But *are* you anybody? . . . Do – *do* tell me who you are!" ' (ch. XXVII). And again, ' "If you really are the nobody I once thought you, you must be a cool hand" ' (ch. XXVII). A cool hand indeed; for Lucy's invisibility is a calculated deception – a blank screen on which others project their view of her. To Graham Bretton she is 'a being inoffensive as a shadow': to M. Paul, denouncing her in a melodramatic hiss, she is dangerously, sexually, insurgent – ' "vous avez l'air bien triste, soumise, rêveuse, mais vous ne l'êtes pas . . . Sauvage! la flamme à l'âme, l'éclair aux yeux!" ' (ch. XXVII).

Actor/spectator: Lucy withholds her true identity from us as well as from the characters whose presence as actors in the novel defines her absence. The most disconcerting of her reticences, and the least functional, concerns her recognition of the medical attendant at the Rue Fossette (Dr John) as Graham Bretton. The 'idea, new, sudden, and startling' (ch. X) which strikes Lucy as she observes him one day at the Pensionnat Beck is not disclosed to the reader until her return to the scene of her and Paulina's childhood love, the reconstituted Bretton household: 'I first recognised him on that occasion, noted several chapters back. . . To *say* anything on the subject, to *hint* at my discovery, had not suited my habit of thought' (ch. XVI). Instead of declaring herself, Lucy prefers to retain her social invisibility – at this stage she is still employed as a nursery-governess. Her strategic silence conceals the private life which Mme Beck's system of surveillance is at pains to detect, while she herself sets about detecting the clandestine flirtation between Dr John ('Isadore', in this role) and Ginevra, much as she had earlier observed the love-game between Graham and the infant Paulina. The novel is full of such voyeurisms (Mme Beck herself is scarcely more on the watch than Lucy) – exhibitions in which Lucy casts herself as an onlooker, passive yet all-powerful. Even when she takes the stage herself, during the school play of chapter XIV, she contrives to combine the two roles – at once spectator and participant in the sexual drama which she enacts between 'Isadore', Ginevra, and her gallant, de Hamal (between the 'Ours' or sincere lover, the coquette, and the fop whose part Lucy plays). Here the divide between stage and audience, watcher and watched, is piquantly removed in the interests of a more complex and ambiguous drama; Lucy also crosses the sexual divide – impersonating a man while clad as a woman from the waist down. In the same way, the *frisson* lies in Lucy's non-subservience to her spectator role, as the game of master/slave in *Jane Eyre* is spiced by Jane's insubordination to her master. Jane discovers a taste for sexual mastery in preference to the more conventional role of mistress: Lucy discovers in herself 'a keen relish for dramatic expression' and, carried away by she knows not what, transforms her part into an unorthodox piece of inter-sexual rivalry – 'I acted to please myself' (ch. XIV).

Vashti: 'but it would not do for a mere looker-on at life' (ch. XIV). Lucy's invisibility is an aspect of her oppression: the actress, Vashti, is an aspect of her hidden revolt. As a middle-class woman, Lucy can only be employed within the home or its educational colony, the school; but that 'home', since she is employee not 'mistress', must remain alien. Though increasingly professionalised, the role of teacher retains many of the anomalies of the governess-figure in her differing guises (mother-substitute, educator, companion). The governess is peculiarly the victim of middle-class sexual ideology, for the only role open to her is that of bringing up children while marriage and motherhood themselves are paradoxically tabooed to her within the family which employs her. Economically non-negotiable (non-exchangeable), she is denied both social and sexual recognition: 'No one knows exactly how to treat her.'[6] Significantly, Lucy prefers the relative independence of remaining a teacher in Mme Beck's pensionnat to Mr Home's offer of employment as Paulina's companion; while Mme Beck sees in Lucy's bid to marry M. Paul a threat to the economic and family interests on which her establishment is founded (Lucy will ultimately set up a rival school). Charlotte Brontë's letters have much to say both about the 'condition of woman' question and about being a governess; but this, finally, of the woman whose destiny is to be unmarried:

> when patience had done its utmost and industry its best, whether in the case of women or operatives, and when both are baffled, and pain and want triumph, the sufferer is free, is entitled, at last to send up to Heaven any piercing cry for relief, if by that he can hope to obtain succour.[7]

In *Villette*, that piercing cry is uttered by an actress whose release of 'hunger, rebellion and rage' sets the theatre literally alight with its revolutionary force. Vashti is a female version of the central Romantic protagonist, the satanic rebel and fallen angel whose damnation is a function of divine tyranny (Blake's Urizen, Byron's Jehovah of sacrifices, Shelley's Jupiter):

> Pain, for her, has no result in good; tears water no harvest of wisdom: on sickness, on death itself, she looks with the eye of a rebel. Wicked, perhaps, she is, but also she is strong; and her strength has conquered Beauty, has overcome Grace, and bound both at her side, captives peerlessly fair, and docile as fair. Even in the uttermost frenzy of energy is each maenad movement royally, imperially, incedingly upborne. Her hair, flying loose in revel or war, is still an angel's hair, and glorious under a halo. Fallen, insurgent, banished, she remembers the heaven where she rebelled. Heaven's light, following her exile, pierces its confines, and discloses their forlorn remoteness.
>
> (ch. XXIII)

Villette can only be silent about the true nature and origin of Lucy's oppression; like Charlotte Brontë's letters, it never questions the enshrining of marriage within Victorian sexual ideology, nor pursues its economic and social consequences for women. But what the novel cannot say is eloquently inscribed in its subtext – in the 'discursive' activity of Lucy's (over-) heated imagination, and in the agitated notation and heightened language which signal it. Here her mingled identification, revulsion and admiration are tellingly juxtaposed with Graham Bretton's indifference to the spectacle. We witness not only his lack of affinity 'for what belonged to storm, what was wild and intense, dangerous, sudden, and flaming' – for the Romantic mode which defines Lucy's own insurgent inner life; we witness also his sexual judgement on 'a woman, not an artist: it was a branding judgement' (ch. XXIII). 'Branded' as a fallen woman, a rebel against conventional morality, Vashti is at once *declassée* and thereby permitted to retain her potency – a daemonic symbol of sexual energy created by a woman (actress/author) in contrast to the static, male-fabricated images of woman exhibited for Lucy's inspection in an earlier chapter: Cleopatra on one hand, the *Jeune Fille/Mariée/Jeune Mère/Veuve* (ch. XIX) on the other (woman as sexual object or as bearer of ideology). 'Where was the artist of the Cleopatra? Let *him* come and sit down and study this different vision' (ch. XXIII; my italics), demands Lucy – in whose scandalous pink dress M. Paul detects a latent scarlet woman.

Heimlich/unheimlich: '*heimlich* is a word the meaning of which develops in the direction of ambivalence, until it finally coincides with its opposite, *unheimlich*.' Thus Freud, for whom the uncanny in fiction provided 'a much more fertile province than the uncanny in real life, for it contains the whole of the latter and something more besides'.[8] Lucy's dream-like propulsion from one world to another – from her childhood at Bretton, to Miss Marchmont's sick-room, to the Pensionnat Beck, and back again to Bretton – makes resourceful use of this fertile province, suspending the laws of probability for those of the mind. Narrative dislocation in *Villette* insists on the irreducible otherness, the strangeness and arbitrariness, of inner experience. Lucy's return to the past (or the return of her past?) is ushered in by a nightmare of estrangement – 'Methought the well-loved dead ... met me elsewhere, alienated' (ch. XV) – and she recovers consciousness after her desperate visit to the confessional amidst the décor of the *unheimliche*: 'all my eye rested on struck it as spectral', 'These articles of furniture could not be real, solid arm-chairs, looking-glasses, and wash-stands – they must be the ghosts of such articles' (ch. XVI). The real becomes spectral, the past alien, the familiar strange; the lost home (*heimlich*) and the uncanny (*unheimlich*) coincide. Like Vashti, Lucy is an exile from the paradisal world of Bretton; even when restored miraculously to it, she cannot remain there. Its true inmate is not the satanic rebel and fallen angel, but the angelic, spiritualised Paulina – whose surname, appropriately, is Home. By marrying her (it is she whom he rescues from the threatened conflagration in the theatre) Graham Bretton ensures the continuation of the *status quo*. But their conventional love-story – child-bride taken in charge by father-substitute – is upstaged by Lucy's more innovatory and disturbing inner drama. In this internal-ised theatre, the part that doubles Lucy's is taken by a (supposed) ghost. Freud's essay on the uncanny offers a classic formulation of Gothic strategy: 'the writer creates a kind of uncertainty in us ... b꜠ not letting us know, no doubt purposely, whether he is taking us ꞉ the real world or into a purely fantastic one of his own creatio꜠ effect of this uncertainty in Charlotte Brontë's novel is tꞈ the monopolistic claims of realism on 'reality' – ꞌ representations no less fictive and arbitrary than Romantic modes usually viewed as parasitic. ꞉ suggests, a peculiarly powerful effect is achꞌ pretends to move in the world of commoꞈ it, 'betraying us to the superstitiousnꞈ surmounted'.[9] The grudge which we is just that retained by readers and critꞈ of the Rue Fossette – in whom repressꞈ

unacknowledged phantom of feminism combine to subvert the novel's façade of realism.

The nun: a realist reading of *Villette* must relegate the nun to the level of Gothic machinery; indicatively, both Kate Millett (for whom the novel is a manifesto of sexual politics) and Terry Eagleton (for whom it is a Marxist myth of power) ignore her ambiguous presence.[10] But just because the device is so cumbrous and unnecessary in realist terms – Ginevra's gallant dressed up for their clandestine assignations – it must have another function. In effect, it symbolises not only Lucy's repression, but the novelist's freedom to evoke or inhibit the *unheimliche*; to lift or impose censorship. The nun thus becomes that phantom or psychic reality which representation represses, evading the censorship of realism as de Hamal himself evades the forbidden ground of the Pensionnat Beck under Mme Beck's censoring eyes. In his medical capacity, Graham Bretton diagnoses 'a case of spectral illusion ... resulting from long-continued mental conflict' (ch. XXII). But as it turns out, the rationalist explanation is debunked by the fictive reality of the novel itself: 'doctors are so self-opinionated, so immovable in their dry, materialist views' (ch. XXIII), Lucy comments with apparent perversity; yet the text vindicates her. The legend of the nun, buried alive in a vault under the Methuselah pear-tree 'for some sin against her vow' (ch. XII), is introduced early on but lies dormant until passion threatens to reassert itself. The first apparition – summoned up, it seems, by Lucy's love for Graham Bretton – occurs when she plunges into the vault-like depths of 'the deep, black, cold garret' (ch. XXII) to enjoy his precious letter:

> Are there wicked things, not human, which envy human bliss? Are there evil influences haunting the air, and poisoning it for man? What was near me? ...
> Something in that vast solitary garret sounded strangely. Most surely and certainly I heard, as it seemed, a stealthy foot on that floor: a sort of gliding out from the direction of the black recess haunted by the malefactor cloaks. I turned: my light was dim; the room was long – but, as I live! I saw in the middle of that ghostly chamber a figure all black or white; the skirts straight, narrow, black; the head bandaged, veiled, white.
> Say what you will, reader – tell me I was nervous, or mad; affirm that I was unsettled by the excitement of that letter; declare that I dreamed: this I vow – I saw there – in that room – on that night – an image like – a NUN.
>
> (ch. XXII)

The sheerest melodrama? or a bold refutation of 'common reality'?
Lucy's challenge – 'Say what you will, reader' – defies us to find the
narrative incredible or the author unreliable. For the reader, there is
no knowing how to take the nun; is Lucy deceiving us again? A brief
admonitory sighting marks her visit to the theatre (an unexplained
light in the *grenier*); but the next full apparition occurs at a similar
moment of high emotional significance – on the still, dim, electric
evening when she buries her letters from Graham, and her love for
him, in a hole under the Methuselah pear-tree:

> the moon, so dim hitherto, seemed to shine out somewhat brighter: a
> ray gleamed even white before me, and a shadow became distinct and
> marked. I looked more narrowly, to make out the cause of this well-
> defined contrast appearing a little suddenly in the obscure alley: whiter
> and blacker it grew on my eye: it took shape with instantaneous
> transformation. I stood about three yards from a tall, sable-robed,
> snowy-veiled woman.
>
> Five minutes passed. I neither fled nor shrieked. She was there still. I
> spoke.
>
> 'Who are you? and why do you come to me?'
>
> (ch. XXVI)

Lucy here both hides a treasure and entombs a grief; does the nun
confront her to assert their kinship? The third apparition – aroused
to vengeful anger – is provoked by M. Paul's declaration of affinity
between himself and Lucy ('"we are alike – there is affinity. Do
you see it mademoiselle, when you look in the glass?"'). The birth
of love and the turbulent re-activation of repression occur simultaneously:

> Yes; there scarce stirred a breeze, and that heavy tree was convulsed,
> whilst the feathery shrubs stood still. For some minutes amongst the
> wood and leafage a rending and heaving went on. Dark as it was, it
> seemed to me that something more solid than either night-shadow, or
> branch-shadow, blackened out of the boles. At last the struggle ceased.
> What birth succeeded this travail? What Dryad was born of these
> throes? We watched fixedly. A sudden bell rang in the house – the
> prayer-bell. Instantly into our alley there came . . . an apparition, all
> black and white. With a sort of angry rush – close, close past our faces
> – swept swiftly the very NUN herself! Never had I seen her so clearly.
> She looked tall of stature, and fierce of gesture. As she went, the wind
> rose sobbing; the rain poured wild and cold; the whole night seemed
> to feel her.
>
> (ch. XXXI)

Natural and supernatural are brought ambiguously into play; the nun is at once 'solid', material, and capable of bringing about changes in the weather – 'betraying us to the superstitiousness we have ostensibly surmounted'.

Mirror, mirror. . . : Lucy's question (' "Who are you?" ') remains unanswered, but the nun's ambiguous status – at once real and spectral, both a deceit practised on Lucy and her psychic double – has important implications for the system of representation employed in the novel. The configuration of characters around Lucy is equally expressive of her quest for identity and of her self-estrangement. Mrs Bretton, Mme Beck, Ginevra, the detestable Zélie of St Pierre and the adorable Paulina are the images of women (the good and bad mothers, the rivals and sisters) through whom Lucy both defines and fails to recognise herself, placed as she is at the centre of a distorting hall of mirrors in which each projection is obedient to her feelings of gratitude, rivalry, attraction, hatred or envy. No other woman in the novel has any identity except as Lucy herself bestows it. The absent centre exerts a centripetal force on the other characters, making them all facets of the consciousness whose passions animate them. And yet this is the level which a realist reading of *Villette* would claim as stable, objective, autonomous, in contrast to the phantasmal subjective world represented by the nun and the Gothic hinterland to which she belongs. At this point one must acknowledge the powerful presence of fantasy in Charlotte Brontë's fiction. M. Paul, no less than Lucy's rivals (the images to whom she must submit or over whom she may triumph), is animated by a wish-fulfilment which it is surely justifiable to see as Charlotte Brontë's own. But far from detracting from the fiction, the release of fantasy both energises *Villette* and satisfies that part of the reader which also desires constantly to reject reality for the sake of an obedient, controllable, narcissistically pleasurable image of self and its relation to the world. From the scene in which Ginevra triumphantly contrasts herself and Lucy in the mirror (ch. XIV), to Lucy's unexpected glimpse of herself in public with Graham Bretton and his mother ('a third person in a pink dress and black lace mantle . . . it might have been worse' [ch. XX]), to M. Paul's declaration of affinity (' "Do you see it . . . when you look in the glass? Do you observe that your forehead is shaped like mine – that your eyes are cut like mine?" ' [ch. XXXI]), we trace, not so much the rehabilitation of the plain heroine, as the persistence of the Lacanian 'Mirror-phase'.[11] Or, to put it in terms of text rather than plot, we too are confronted by an image in which

signifier and signified have imaginary correspondence – by a seductive representational illusion which denies the lack or absence central
to all signification. The nun stands opposed to this imaginary
plenitude of sign or image. Too easily identified as the spectre of
repression, or as the double of Lucy's repressed self, she is none the
less recalcitrantly other; ' "Who are you?" ', asks Lucy, not recognising her. She is the joker in the pack, the alien, ex-centric self which no
image can mirror – only the structure of language. Like the purloined
letter in Lacan's reading of the Poe story, where the meaning of the
letter (the autonomous signifier) lies in its function in the plot rather
than its actual contents, the nun derives her significance from her
place in the signifying chain.[12] She has one function in relation to
Lucy, another in relation to M. Paul, and another again in relation to
Ginevra. The different meanings intersect but do not merge; the
threads cross and intertwine without becoming one. Her uncanniness
lies in unsettling the 'mirroring' conventions of representation present elsewhere in *Villette*, and in validating Gothic and Romantic
modes, not as 'discursive' and parasitic, but – because shifting,
unstable, arbitrary and dominated by desire – as the system of
signification which can more properly articulate the self.

   The TRUTH: so what are we to make of Lucy's extraordinary
narrative? which level of the text finally claims priority? Pursuit of
the nun to the novel's climax – the phantasmagoric scenes of Lucy's
drugged nocturnal expedition to the illuminated park – provides an
answer of sorts. The nun has by this time manifested herself in
another guise, as the external obstacle to marriage between Lucy and
M. Paul; that is, his supposed devotion to the dead, sainted Justine
Marie (and, with her, to Roman Catholicism) whose nun-like portrait
is pointedly exhibited to Lucy by Père Silas, as well as his guardianship of a bouncing, all-too-alive ward of the same name. Her
presence at the climax of the novel perfectly illustrates Charlotte
Brontë's deviousness, the strategy by which her heroine's consciousness at once distorts, and, in doing so, creates a truth that is
essentially a fiction. In this coda-like sequence, all the characters of
the novel are paraded before the apparently invisible Lucy in their
happy family parties – the Brettons and Homes; the Becks, Père Silas
and Mme Walravens; and lastly, after an elaborate build-up of
expectation and delay, M. Paul and his ward. Thus Lucy is ostensibly
returned to her original role of excluded spectator. But there is a
difference. This time it is she who is *metteur en scène* in a drama of
her own making. First comes 'the crisis and the revelation', the long-

awaited arrival of the nun or her double, Justine Marie – heightened
by Lucy's anticipatory memories of her earlier hauntings:

> It is over. The moment and the nun are come. The crisis and the
> revelation are passed by.
> The flambeau glares still within a yard, held up in a park-keeper's
> hand; its long eager tongue of flame almost licks the figure of the
> Expected – there – where she stands full in my sight! What is she like?
> What does she wear? How does she look? Who is she?
> There are many masks in the Park to-night, and as the hour wears
> late, so strange a feeling of revelry and mystery begins to spread
> abroad that scarce would you discredit me, reader, were I to say that
> she is like the nun of the attic, that she wears black skirts and white
> head-clothes, that she looks the resurrection of the flesh, and that she
> is a risen ghost.
> All falsities – all figments! We will not deal in this gear. Let us be
> honest, and cut, as heretofore, from the homely web of truth.
> *Homely*, though, is an ill-chosen word. What I see is not precisely
> homely. A girl of Villette stands there . . .
>
> (ch. XXXIX)

'*Heimlich* is a word the meaning of which develops in the direction
of ambivalence . . .' Once again it is the living not the dead, the
familiar not the strange, that becomes uncanny; not least because
the bathos fails to proceed as expected. Instead, the transformation
of spectral nun into bourgeois belle is followed by yet another
audacious reversal – a denial of reality whereby Lucy invents an
engagement between M. Paul and his ward, a fiction whose basis
('his nun was indeed buried') is the truth of her own autonomous
imagination:

> Thus it must be. The revelation was indeed come. Presentiment had
> not been mistaken in her impulse; there is a kind of presentiment
> which never *is* mistaken; it was I who had for a moment miscalcu-
> lated; not seeing the true bearing of the oracle, I had thought she
> muttered of vision when, in truth, her prediction touched reality.
> I might have paused longer upon what I saw; I might have
> deliberated ere I drew inferences. Some perhaps would have held the
> premises doubtful, the proofs insufficient; some slow sceptics would
> have incredulously examined, ere they conclusively accepted the
> project of a marriage between a poor and unselfish man of forty, and
> his wealthy ward of eighteen; but far from me such shifts and
> palliatives, far from me such temporary evasion of the actual, such
> coward fleeing from the dread, the swift-footed, the all-overtaking
> Fact, such feeble suspense of submission to her the sole sovereign, such

paltering and faltering resistance to the Power whose errand is to
march conquering and to conquer, such traitor defection from the
TRUTH.

(ch. XXXIX)

Is this Lucy's final and most outrageous lie? or, as the text insists in
the face of its heavily alliterative irony, the novel's central 'truth'? –
that the imagination usurps on the real to create its own fictions; that
Lucy is essentially and inevitably single. Meanwhile, the self-
torturing narrative and masochistic imagery ('I invoked Conviction
to nail upon me the certainty, abhorred while embraced') speed her
back to her solitary dormitory in the Rue Fossette, to the effigy of the
nun on her bed, and the empty garments which signal 'the resurrection of the flesh':

> Tempered by late incidents, my nerves disdained hysteria. Warm from
> illuminations, and music, and thronging thousands, thoroughly lashed
> up by a new scourge, I defied spectra. In a moment, without
> exclamation, I had rushed on the haunted couch; nothing leaped out,
> or sprung, or stirred; all the movement was mine, so was all the life,
> the reality, the substance, the force; as my instinct felt. I tore her up –
> the incubus! I held her on high – the goblin! I shook her loose – the
> mystery! And down she fell – down all round me – down in shreds
> and fragments – and I trode upon her.

(ch. XXXIX)

The phrasing is odd and significant: 'all the movement was mine, so
was all the life, the reality, the substance, the force.' The wardrobe
mockingly bequeathed to Lucy by the eloped Ginevra and de Hamal
labels her as the nun of the Rue Fossette – at once accusing her of
animating the spectre from within herself, and forcing her to
recognise its true identity.

   The double ending: but of course the narrative doesn't leave things
there, although the ambiguous ending cunningly attempts to do so –
at once uniting Lucy and M. Paul in their educational idyll, and
severing them for ever. The final evasion ('Trouble no quiet, kind
heart; leave sunny imaginations hope' [ch. XLII]) was clearly
designed to satisfy the conventional novel-reader as well as Charlotte
Brontë's father. But there is more to it. Of the two letters she writes
to Graham Bretton, Lucy tells us: 'To speak truth, I compromised
matters; I served two masters: I bowed down in the house of
Rimmon, and lifted the heart at another shrine' (ch. XXIII). The
entire novel, not just its ending, bears the marks of this compromise

– between Victorian romance and the Romantic Imagination, between the realist novel and Gothicism. The relationship between the two texts is as arbitrary as that between the two letters; as the signified slides under the signifier, so the buried letter bears an excentric relation to the public version. This is not to say that the real meaning of *Villette*, 'the TRUTH', lies in its ghostly subtext. Rather, the relationship between the two points to what the novel cannot say about itself – to the real conditions of its literary possibility. Instead of correcting the novel into a false coherence, we should see in its ruptured and ambiguous discourse the source of its uncanny power. The double ending, in reversing the truth/fiction hierarchy, not only reinstates fantasy as a dominant rather than parasitic version of reality, but at the same time suggests that there can be no firm ground; only a perpetual de-centring activity. Fittingly, the sleight of hand is carried out with the aid of metaphors drawn from the Romantic paradox of creation-in-destruction. The tempest by which Lucy's earliest loss is signified becomes an apocalyptic upheaval prophesying rebirth as well as death when the time comes for her to leave Miss Marchmont ('disturbed volcanic action . . . rivers suddenly rushing above their banks . . . strange high tides flowing furiously in on low sea-coasts' (ch. IV]). In the same way, Lucy's loss of consciousness before her rebirth into the Bretton household, later in the novel, is heralded by renewed images of Shelleyan storm – 'I only wished that I had wings and could ascend the gale, spread and repose my pinions on its strength, career in its course, sweep where it swept' (ch. XV). There is thus a profound ambiguity in the Romantic cataclysm which shipwrecks Lucy's happiness at the end of the novel:

> The skies hang full and dark – a rack sails from the west; the clouds cast themselves into strange forms – arches and broad radiations; there rise resplendent mornings – glorious, royal, purple as monarch in his state; the heavens are one flame; so wild are they, they rival battle at its thickest – so bloody, they shame Victory in her pride. I know some signs of the sky; I have noted them ever since childhood. God, watch that sail! Oh! guard it!
>
> . . .
>
> That storm roared frenzied for seven days. It did not cease till the Atlantic was strewn with wrecks: it did not lull till the deeps had gorged their full of sustenance. Not till the destroying angel of tempest had achieved his perfect work, would he fold the wings whose waft was thunder – the tremor of whose plumes was storm.
> (ch. XLII)

John Martin and the Angel of Death transform Lucy's premonition of loss into an apocalyptic victory of the imagination. By admitting to the incompatibility of the world of thought and the world of reality, Lucy at last becomes a truly reliable narrator – single and double at the same time. And by tacitly affirming the centrality of shipwreck, loss and deprivation to the workings of her imagination, Charlotte Brontë also reveals the deepest sources of her own creativity.

The anxiety of influence: Harold Bloom would presumably see the nun as an emblem of repression in a belated text whose sexual anguish, like that of Tennyson's 'Mariana', masks influence-anxiety (note the analogous presence of the Methuselah pear-tree and the famous poplar).[13] A plausible case could be made for misreading *Villette* in the same way. Charlotte Brontë's imagination was nurtured on Romanticism ('that burning clime where we have sojourned too long – its skies flame – the glow of sunset is always upon it'),[14] but the world of Angria had to be repressed in the interests of Victorian realism: 'When I first began to write ... I restrained imagination, eschewed romance, repressed excitement.'[15] It was no more possible to write a Romantic novel in the mid-nineteenth century than to read one, as the bewildered and imperceptive reviews of *Wuthering Heights* reveal. Unlike her sister, Emily Brontë refused to bow down in the house of Rimmon, and in an important sense, hers is the repressed presence in *Villette*. Lucy's unwilling return to consciousness in the Bretton household ('Where my soul went during that swoon I cannot tell ... She may have gone upward, and come in sight of her eternal home ... I know she re-entered her prison with pain, with reluctance' [ch. XVI]) resembles nothing so much as Emily Brontë's 'Prisoner' after visionary flight: 'Oh, dreadful is the check – intense the agony/When the ear begins to hear and the eye begins to see ...'[16] Her invocation 'To Imagination' underlies *Villette*'s paeon to the Imagination in the face of Reason's tyranny ('"But if I feel, may I *never* express?" "*Never!*" declared Reason' [ch. XXI]). Emily Brontë had written, 'So hopeless is the world without,/The world within I doubly prize', and welcomed a 'benignant power,/Sure solacer of human cares' –

> Reason indeed may oft complain
> For Nature's sad reality,
> And tell the suffering heart how vain
> Its cherished dreams must always be;
> And Truth may rudely trample down
> The flowers of Fancy newly blown.

> But thou art ever there to bring
> The hovering visions back and breathe
> New glories o'er the blighted spring
> And call a lovelier life from death,
> And whisper with a voice divine
> Of real worlds as bright as thine.[17]

Charlotte Brontë, in turn, creates one of the most remarkable invocations to Imagination in Victorian literature – a passage that criticism of *Villette* has proved consistently unable to assimilate, or even acknowledge:

> Often has Reason turned me out by night, in mid-winter, on cold snow. . . . Then, looking up, have I seen in the sky a head amidst circling stars, of which the midmost and the brightest lent a ray sympathetic and attent. A spirit, softer and better than Human Reason, has descended with quiet flight to the waste – bringing all round her a sphere of air borrowed of eternal summer; bringing perfume of flowers which cannot fade – fragrance of trees whose fruit is life; bringing breezes pure from a world whose day needs no sun to lighten it. My hunger has this good angel appeased with food, sweet and strange, gathered amongst gleaming angels. . . . Divine, compassionate, succourable influence! When I bend the knee to other than God, it shall be at thy white and winged feet, beautiful on mountain or on plain. Temples have been reared to the Sun – altars dedicated to the Moon. Oh, greater glory! To thee neither hands build, nor lips consecrate; but hearts, through ages, are faithful to thy worship. A dwelling thou hast, too wide for walls, too high for dome – a temple whose floors are space – rites whose mysteries transpire in presence, to the kindling, the harmony of worlds!
>
> (ch. XXI)

The dizzying and visionary prose strains, like Shelley's poetry, away from the actual towards enkindled abstractions that image the human mind. But the deity that the temple of the heart enshrines is female; like the embodiment of rebellion and rage (Vashti), the spirit that succours the mind's hunger has been triumphantly feminised.

Feminism and Romanticism: 'nothing but hunger, rebellion and rage. . . . No fine writing can hide this thoroughly, and it will be fatal to her in the long run' – Arnold's prognosis was wrong (Charlotte Brontë died of pregnancy), but revealingly poses a split between rebellion and 'fine writing'. The divorce of the Romantic Imagination from its revolutionary impulse poses special problems for Victorian Romantics. Where vision had once meant a prophetic denunciation

of the *status quo* and the imagining of radical alternatives, it comes
to threaten madness or mob-violence. Losing its socially transform-
ing role, it can only turn inwards to self-destructive solipsism.
Charlotte Brontë's own mistrust erupts in *Villette* with the fire that
flames out during Vashti's performance or in the long-vacation
nightmare which drives Lucy to the confessional; while the spectral
nun (the Alastor of the Rue Fossette?) has to be laid in order to free
Lucy from the burden of the autonomous imagination and allow her
to become an economically independent headmistress. There are
added complications for a woman writer. The drive to female
emancipation, while fuelled by revolutionary energy, had an ultimately conservative aim – successful integration into existing social
structures (' "I am a rising character: once an old lady's companion,
then a nursery-governess, now a school-teacher" ', Lucy tells Ginevra
ironically [ch. XXVII]). Moreover, while the novel's pervasive femin-
isation of the Romantic Imagination is a triumph, it runs the
attendant risk of creating a female ghetto. The annexing of special
powers of feeling and intuition to women and its consequences (their
relegation to incompetent dependency) has an equally strong Romantic
tradition; women, idiots and children, like the debased version of the
Romantic poet, become at once privileged and (legally) irresponsible.
The problem is illuminated by situating Charlotte Brontë's novels
within a specifically feminist tradition. *Villette*'s crushing opposition
between Reason and Imagination is also present in Mary Wollstonecraft's writing. *The Rights of Woman* (1791) – directed against
the infantilising Rousseauist ideal of feminine 'sensibility' – not only
advocates the advantages for women of a rational (rather than
sentimental) education, but attempts to insert the author herself into
the predominantly male discourse of Enlightenment Reason, or 'sense'.
Yet, paradoxically, it is within this shaping Rousseauist sensibility
that Mary Wollstonecraft operates as both woman and writer –
creating in her two highly autobiographical novels, *Mary* (1788) and
The Wrongs of Woman (1798), fictions which, even as they anato-
mise the constitution of femininity within the confines of 'sensibility',
cannot escape its informing preoccupations and literary influence.[18]
Though their concepts of Reason differ, the same split is felt by
Charlotte Brontë. In *Villette*, Reason is the wicked and 'envenomed'
step-mother as opposed to the succouring, nourishing, consoling
'daughter of heaven', Imagination (ch. XXI). It is within this primal
yet divisive relationship that the novelist herself is constituted as
woman and writer – nurtured on Romanticism, fostered by uncon-

genial Reason. The duality haunts her novel, dividing it as Lucy is divided against herself.

Feminist criticism/feminist critic: it is surely no longer the case, as Kate Millett asserts, that literary criticism of the Brontës is 'a long game of masculine prejudice wherein the player either proves they can't write and are hopeless primitives . . . or converts them into case histories from the wilds'.[19] But feminist criticism still has a special task in relation to Charlotte Brontë's novels. That task is not to explain away, but to explain – to theorise – the incoherencies and compromises, inconsistencies and dislocations, which provoked the 'can't write' jibe in the first place; to suggest, in other words, the source of Matthew Arnold's disquiet. It is enough to point to the part played by realism and Reason respectively in Charlotte Brontë's double quest for literary form and for female emancipation. To do so relocates her writing, not in a neurotic northern hinterland ('case histories from the wilds'), but in the mainstream of Victorian literary production – its legacy of Romanticism complicated in her case by the conflict between a revolutionary impulse towards feminism and its tendency to confine women within irrationality. And what of the feminist critic? Isn't she in the same position as Charlotte Brontë, the writer, and her character, Lucy Snowe? – bound, if she's to gain both a living and a hearing, to install herself within the prevailing conventions of academic literary criticism. To this extent, hers must also be an ex-centric text, a displacement into criticism of the hunger, rebellion and rage which make Lucy an estranged image of self. Constituted within conditions essentially unchanged since those of Mary Wollstonecraft and Charlotte Brontë (i.e. patriarchy) and experiencing similar contradictions within herself and society, the feminist critic faces the same disjunction – removed, however, to the disjunction between literary response and critical discourse. The novel itself becomes the discourse of the Other, making its presence felt in the distortions and mutilations of critical selectivity (*Vashti, The Nun, Feminism and Romanticism*). What strategy remains, beyond unsettling the illusory objectivity of criticism? Surely also to unfold a novel whose very repressions become an eloquent testimony to imaginative freedom, whose ruptures provide access to a double text, and whose doubles animate, as well as haunt, the fiction they trouble. In the last resort, the buried letter of Romanticism and the phantom of feminism both owe their uncanny power to their subterranean and unacknowledged presence – to repression itself, the subject of Charlotte Brontë's most haunting novel, and fiction's special reserve.

From *Women Writing and Writing about Women*, ed. Mary Jacobus
(London, 1979), pp. 42–55, 57–9.

NOTES

[This essay had its origins in a joint paper presented to the Essex Conference
on the Sociology of Literature in 1977 by the Marxist-Feminist Literary
Collective (see 'Women Writing: "Jane Eyre", "Shirley", "Villette",
"Aurora Leigh"' in *1848: The Sociology of Literature*, eds Francis Barker *et
al.* [Colchester, 1978], pp. 185–206). It first appeared separately in *Essays in
Criticism*, vol. xxxix (July, 1978), then in a longer version in *Women
Writing and Writing about Women*, a collection of essays edited by Mary
Jacobus and based largely on a lecture series on Women and Literature
delivered in Oxford in 1978. Jacobus's essay marked an important advance
in the theoretical sophistication of Brontë criticism, particularly in its
application of deconstructive and psychoanalytic theory. In her attention to
the novel's 'ruptured and ambiguous discourse', Jacobus argues that repression
not only provides the subject matter of Brontë's novel but is manifest at a
formal level in the 'inconsistencies and dislocations' in the novel. Ed.]

1. A shortened version of this essay appeared in *Essays in Criticism*, 39
   (July 1978), 228–44. I am grateful to the editors for permission to
   reprint it here, and to the London-based Marxist-Feminist Literary
   Collective for whom an early version was originally written. Quotations
   are from the first editions of Charlotte Brontë's novels; references are to
   chapter divisions.

2. 'The "Uncanny"' (1919) in James Strachey (trans. and ed.), *The
   Standard Edition of the Complete Psychological Works of Sigmund
   Freud* (24 vols, London, 1955), vol. 17, p. 241. See Hélène Cixous's
   seminal 'Fiction and its Phantoms: A Reading of Freud's *Das Unheimliche* (The "uncanny")', *New Literary History*, 7 (1976), 525–48.

3. Matthew Arnold to Mrs Foster, 14 April 1853; see Miriam Allott (ed.),
   The Brontës: The Critical Heritage (London, 1974), p. 201.

4. Kate Millett, *Sexual Politics* (London, 1971), p. 146.

5. To W. S. Williams, 6 November 1852, and George Smith, 3 November
   1852; T. Wise and J. A. Symington (eds), *The Shakespeare Head
   Brontë: The Life and Letters* (4 vols, London, 1932), vol. 4, pp. 18, 16.

6. Elizabeth Sewell, *Principles of Education* (2 vols, London, 1865), vol.
   2, p. 240. See M. J. Peterson, 'The Victorian Governess: Status Incongruence in Family and Society', *Victorian Studies*, 14 (1970), 7–26.

7. To W. S. Williams, 12 May 1848, in *The Shakespeare Head Brontë: The
   Life and Letters*, vol. 2, p. 216.

8. Sigmund Freud, *The Complete Psychological Works of Sigmund Freud*, trans. and ed. James Strachey (London, 1955), vol. 17, pp. 246, 249.

9. Ibid., vol. 17, p. 250.

10. See Kate Millett, *Sexual Politics* (London, 1971), pp. 140–7, and Terry Eagleton, *Myths of Power: A Marxist Study of the Brontës* (London, 1975), pp. 61–73. [For Millett and Eagleton, see pp. 32, 107. Ed.]

11. See Jacques Lacan, *Ecrits*, trans. Alan Sheridan (London, 1977), pp. 1–7.

12. 'Seminar on "The Purloined Letter"', trans. Jeffrey Mehlman, *Yale French Studies*, 48 (1972), 38–72.

13. See Harold Bloom, *Poetry and Repression* (New Haven and London, 1976), pp. 147–54.

14. 'Farewell to Angria', *c.* 1839; see F. E. Ratchford and W. C. De Vane, *Legends of Angria* (New Haven, 1933), p. 316.

15. To G. H. Lewes, 6 November 1847, in *The Shakespeare Head Brontë: The Life and Letters*, vol. 2, p. 152.

16. Emily Brontë, ll. 85–6, no. 190 in C. W. Hatfield (ed.), *The Complete Poems of Emily Jane Brontë* (London, 1941), p. 239.

17. No. 174, ibid., pp. 205–6.

18. See Mary Wollstonecraft, *Mary, a Fiction and the Wrongs of Woman*, ed. Gary Kelly (London, 1976), pp. vii–xxi, and Margaret Walters, 'The Rights and Wrongs of Women', in Juliet Mitchell and Ann Oakley (eds), *The Rights and Wrongs of Women* (London, 1976), pp. 304–29.

19. Kate Millett, *Sexual Politics* (London, 1971), p. 147.

9

'The Surveillance of a Sleepless Eye': the Constitution of Neurosis in 'Villette'

SALLY SHUTTLEWORTH

The fame of the 'mad wife' in *Jane Eyre* has ensured that the writings of Charlotte Brontë are firmly associated in the public mind with a preoccupation with madness. Brontë's interest in the demarcation of insanity is not restricted to this one text but is pursued in her final novel, *Villette*, where the narrator is subject, seemingly, to hallucinations, undergoes a nervous collapse, and discusses her symptoms at great length with a doctor. Despite this foregrounding of medical expertise, no one has, as yet, placed *Villette* in the context of the intense psychological debates conducted in the scientific writings and popular press of the mid-Victorian era.

Insanity and nervous disease were the subject of acute public concern at this time. The mid-century witnessed the founding of public asylums and the professionalisation of the medical treatment of insanity, developments which were accompanied by detailed discussions in the periodical press concerning the functions and processes of the mind. The aim of this essay is to place *Villette* within this social and scientific discourse on psychology, and to analyse the ways in which the novel both absorbs and resists the definitions and codifications of female experience offered by the male medical establishment.

Charlotte Brontë takes as her subject in *Villette* the inner processes of mind of a subject who defines herself, at one stage in her narrative, as 'constitutionally nervous'.[1] When writing *Jane Eyre*, Brontë had deliberately created a split between Jane and her 'dark double'[2] – the concealed and imprisoned 'mad' wife of Rochester – offering, through a process of analogy and contrast, an analysis of the social construction of insanity. In *Villette* she confronts the issue of psychological instability more directly through the figure of her narrator, Lucy Snowe, focusing now, not on the flamboyant extreme of 'mania', but on the more subtle area of the constitution of neurosis. Through the autobiographical account of 'calm', 'shadow-like' Lucy, the archetypal unreliable narrator, Brontë both explores and interrogates contemporary theories of mental alienation.

The text of *Villette* is dominated by the practice of surveillance. The constant self-surveillance and concealment which marks Lucy's own narrative account is figured socially in the institutional practices of those who surround her. All characters spy on others, attempting, covertly, to read and interpret the external signs of faces, minds and actions. Madame Beck runs her school according to the watchwords '"surveillance", "espionage"' (p. 99); M. Paul reads Lucy's countenance on her arrival in Villette, and later studies her through his 'magic lattice'; and Père Silas focuses on her 'the surveillance of a sleepless eye' – the Roman Catholic confessional (p. 592). Lucy is subjected to educational, professional and religious surveillance. Each observer tries to read her inner self through the interpretation of outer signs. This practice takes its most authoritative form in the narrative in the medical judgements of Dr John.

After Lucy's first encounter with the nun, as she is attempting to read Dr John's letter, he in turn tries to 'read' her: 'I look on you now from a professional point of view, and I read, perhaps, all you would conceal – in your eye, which is curiously vivid and restless: in your cheek, which the blood has forsaken; in your hand, which you cannot steady' (p. 355). Dr John directs onto Lucy the gaze of medical authority, calmly confident of his ability to define inner experience from outer signs. His verdict is distinguished by his insistence on his professional status, and by his unshakeable belief that, no matter how hard Lucy might try to hide from his gaze, he would penetrate through to her innermost secrets. The rhetoric of unveiling and penetrating the truth, so prevalent in nineteenth-century science, is here located as a discourse of power: male science unveils female nature.[3]

All those who subject Lucy to surveillance present her with interpretations of her mind and character, but only Dr John claims the authority of science for his interpretation (though M. Paul, to a lesser extent, also assumes this power when he offers a phrenological reading of her skull). Against the descriptive labels offered by Madame Beck and Père Silas, Dr John presents a whole language of analysis and a theory of psychological functioning. His diagnosis on this occasion is that it is 'a matter of the nerves', a 'case of spectral illusion ... following on and resulting from long-continued mental conflict' (pp. 357, 358). The terms of his analysis are drawn directly from contemporary medical science where the subject of 'spectral illusion' proved a constant source of debate.[4] Against more visionary explanations of the nun, who functions as a site of crucial interpretative conflict in the text, he offers a materialist explanation based on the functioning of the nervous system. On one level, the text falsifies Dr John's materialist explanation by presenting an even more material cause – the physical presence of the Count de Hamal masquerading as a nun. The authority of science is not, however, thereby erased from the text. The very inadequacy of the 'literal' explanation, indeed, feeds further speculation into the question of the relationship between body and mind which functions as a subtext in the novel. As readers interpreting the signs of Lucy's discourse, we are constantly tempted by the text into re-enacting the role of Dr John, as we attempt to pierce through the external linguistic signs of the narrative to a concealed unity lying below. The text, however, frustrates all such quests for a hidden unitary meaning, deliberately undermining the social and psychological presuppositions which underlie such a quest.

In focusing interpretative attention in the novel on Lucy's 'sightings' of the nun, Brontë is deliberately raising the issue of Lucy's psychological stability. Hallucinations, as Brontë was clearly aware, were classically regarded as signs of madness.[5] Lucy herself invokes this mode of explanation on her first glimpse of the nun, challenging the reader to say, 'I was nervous, or mad' (p. 351). Despite Lucy's stated resistance to Dr John's system of analysis, she constantly employs contemporary scientific language to describe her own psychological functioning. The term 'nervous system', which she finds alien and technical when used by Dr John, has already figured largely in her narrative (p. 261). Other terms from contemporary scientific discourse, such as 'monomania', 'hypochondria' and 'hysteria' are also employed with precision in her analysis. Scientific

language in the novel is not confined to Dr John's specific diagnoses –
the imposition of 'male reason' on a largely Gothic text – it frames
Lucy's narrative construction of her self.

In order to understand Brontë's explorations of the psyche in
Villette it is essential to place the novel in the context of mid-
nineteenth-century medical and social debate. Unlike her contempor-
aries George Eliot and Wilkie Collins, for instance, who explicitly
recorded their indebtedness to psychological theory, Brontë has not
generally been noted for her interest in this area.[6] Evidence from her
novels and letters, however, which are permeated with contemporary
psychological vocabulary, suggests a rather different picture. The
following analysis will draw on the diverse sources through which
psychological debate penetrated into the Haworth household: local
newspapers, periodicals, texts in the Keighley Mechanics' Institute
Library, and, perhaps most significantly, the Reverend Brontë's
secular bible: Thomas John Graham's *Domestic Medicine*.[7] This
text, which clearly stands behind the authority of Dr John Graham
Bretton, has been annotated throughout by Patrick Brontë, revealing
a wealth of reading in psychological medicine and a personal interest
in nervous diseases (Patrick records his fears concerning his own
psychological health, and the symptoms of Branwell).

The preoccupation with nervous disorder in *Villette* reflects contemporary social concern. The mid-Victorian press was full of
alarmist reports concerning supposed dramatic increases in the
numbers of the insane, while the borders between sanity and insanity
also seemed to be called into question. As a writer observed in *The
Times*, July 1853, 'Nothing can be more slightly defined than the
line of demarcation between sanity and insanity. ... Make the
definition too narrow, it becomes meaningless; make it too wide, the
whole human race are involved in the drag-net.'[8] The observation
reflects the radical shift in social attitudes toward insanity in the
nineteenth century which culminated in the passing of the two
Lunatic Acts in 1845 and the setting up of public asylums. For the
first time the insane were sharply distinguished from the criminal or
pauper. This development was directly related, however, to the rise
of theories of 'moral management' for the treatment of the insane,
which stressed the recuperability of the mentally ill, thus breaking
down any absolute barrier between sanity and insanity.[9] While
earlier theorists had tended to stress the animal nature of the insane,
the moral managers stressed their membership in a common humanity.
Thus at the same time that insanity was being constructed as a

distinct social category, the borders separating it from sanity were also being eroded.

The social and institutional change signalled by the founding of the public asylums was underpinned by the growing professionalisation of medical practice, and by the growth of a new specialty – alienism, or psychological medicine. Doctors henceforth claimed the exclusive right to define and treat insanity. Their claims to authority were supported by developments in physiological research which designated the brain and nervous system as the site of mental life.[10] The social and philosophical debate concerning the constitution of the self is crystallised in each era in the discussion of insanity. . . . The crucial term in pre-1860s debate was control. At the same time that the popular and scientific press offered increasing numbers of articles on dreams, apparitions, and the operations of the unconscious mind, the dominant ideology remained that of self-control, as exemplified in John Barlow's work entitled *Man's Power over Himself to Prevent or Control Insanity* (1843). Popular response to mesmerism underlined this duality. Thus one critic could account for the attraction of mesmerism in terms only of an 'imbecility of the nervous system, a ready abandonment of the will, a facility in relinquishing every endowment which makes man *human*'.[11] Fear of the loss of control, of public exposure, underlies this attack. Emphasis on an individual's necessary responsibility for action is coupled with an overwhelming sense that control is at every moment liable to be overthrown.

The nineteenth-century preoccupation with control has been linked, by Andrew Scull, to the economic nexus. The shift in the treatment of the insane, as the external mechanisms of restraint of whips and chains were replaced by an emphasis on internal control and the inner discipline of the mind, was directly related, he argues, to the rise of laissez-faire economics: lunatics, like the industrial workforce, had to be taught the principles of ' "rational" self-interest' which governed the marketplace.[12] The individualist philosophy encapsulated in Samuel Smiles's notion of 'self-help' governed the treatment of the insane. The asylum formed a microcosm of Victorian society: social and psychological ordering was achieved through constant surveillance, or 'careful watching', and its psychological reflex, the internalisation of social controls.[13]

Women held a different relationship to this system from men: the medical construction of categories of insanity reinforced the sexual stereotypes of social discourse.[14] The debates concerning self-control were underpinned by the traditional nature-culture polarity; women were assimilated to the side of nature. . . . As the pre-eminent theorist of insanity, Esquirol, observed: 'Physical causes act more frequently upon women than men.'[15] Menstruation, childbirth, lactation, all contributed to the myth of 'feminine vulnerability': women were seen to possess a biological predisposition to insanity. The social construction of women, which endowed them with feeling, but little reason, also thereby reduced their capacity to resist the onslaughts of the body. Thus at the same time that the Victorian social code ruthlessly enforced ideas of 'modesty' and 'decorum' in female behaviour, it also presented women with an image of their own powerlessness actively to achieve these qualities. In the mid-century criminal trial, where insanity had come to be a recognised plea, women, like children and idiots, were held to be not 'responsible' for their actions.[16]

The success of this medicosocial constitution of the feminine can be judged, as Showalter has observed, by the evident collusion of middle-class women in this process: 'how eagerly they embraced insanity as an explanation of their unfeminine impulses, and welcomed the cures that would extinguish the forbidden throb of sexuality or ambition.'[17] In analysis of *Villette*, I will be concerned to examine how far Lucy Snowe, in constructing her narrative, resists such collusion, and how far she recapitulates the definitions and codifications of female experience offered by the male medical establishment.

Brontë's depiction of Lucy's life shows clearly how institutional practices of surveillance are inscribed within the self. Medical surveillance is matched by Madame Beck's professional control, which Lucy relates directly to the practices of industry, referring to her 'system of managing and regulating this mass of machinery' (p. 99). Madame Beck's machine seems to function independently of any personal intervention, operating rather on the participant's internalisation of the mechanisms of control. As Foucault observes of the principles of Bentham's Panopticon (which he takes as paradigmatic of nineteenth-century modes of social control), 'He who is subjected to a field of visibility, and who knows it, assumes responsibility for the constraints of power; he makes them play spontaneously upon himself; he inscribes in himself the power relation in which he simultaneously plays both roles; he becomes the principle of his own subjection.'[18] Lucy clearly demonstrates this psychological pattern, allowing all her actions to be dictated by the sense that she might be overlooked. Thus at one stage she even invests inanimate nature with the qualities of spy: 'the eyes of the flowers had gained vision, and the knots in the tree-boles listened like secret ears' (p. 161).

The third form of surveillance to which Lucy is subject is that of the Roman Catholic church. Her impulse to confession – the voluntary revelation of the secrets of the inner self – represents for Lucy the nadir of her mental state. Worn out by suffering consequent on her internalisation of the social contradictions of the female role, she sacrifices the last vestiges of her autonomy, thus opening herself up to the continued intervention of both medical and religious authorities in her life (and precipitating her entry into the 'very safe asylum' offered by the Brettons) (p. 244). Père Silas proves even more assiduous in his 'treatment' than Dr John. From that moment on, as he later informs her, he had not 'for a day lost sight of you, nor for an hour failed to take in you a rooted interest' (p. 571). He envisages her 'passed under the discipline of Rome, moulded by her high training, inoculated with her salutary doctrines' (the manuscript originally read 'sane' doctrines). With its aim of total dominion over the mind through the discipline of its sane/salutary doctrines, Lucy's Roman Catholic church replicates precisely the alientists' system of moral management of the insane.

The perceived threat of the church to Lucy does not end with her confession. As her relationship with Dr John is subject always to the scrutiny of Madame Beck 'glid[ing] ghost-like through the house, watching and spying everywhere' (p. 100), so her relationship with M. Paul is attended by that 'ghostly troubler' (p. 600), Père Silas, and the threat of the confessional: 'We were under the surveillance of a sleepless eye: Rome watched jealously her son through that mystic lattice at which I had knelt once, and to which M. Emanuel drew nigh month by month – the sliding panel of the confessional' (p. 592). Lucy's use of the term 'magic lattice' echoes, significantly, M. Paul's description of his 'post of observation', his window overlooking the garden, where he sits and 'reads' 'female human nature': 'Ah, magic lattice! what miracles of discovery hast thou wrought' (p. 528). The 'magic lattice' forms another medium for the male gaze to penetrate through to the recesses of the female psyche, furnishing information which is then appropriated to judge and censor, in accordance with male definitions of female decorum (M. Paul rejects Zélie St Pierre on the basis of his observations). Lucy herself, M. Paul observes, wants 'checking, regulating, and keeping down'. She needs 'watching, and watching over' (p. 526). Lucy vehemently repudiates M. Paul's methods: 'To study the human heart thus, is to banquet secretly and sacrilegiously on Eve's apples. I wish you were a Protestant' (p. 530). The phrase 'Eve's apples', used in connection with the voyeuristic practice of spying on women, takes on a decisive sexual charge. The implicit connection, made throughout the book, between Roman Catholicism and the threatened exposure, and suppression, of female sexuality is here brought to the surface.

The school legend of the nun 'buried alive, for some sin against her vow' (p. 148) establishes a chain of association between nuns, ghosts and sexuality which reverberates throughout the novel. Lucy, burying her precious letters from Dr John above the nun's grave, is associating the unspecified 'sin' with sexual transgression. Her 'sightings' of the nun occur, significantly, at moments of heightened sexual tension, while the ghostly pursuit to which she is subject seems to embody externally her own activities of self-suppression. Lucy's violent antagonism to Roman Catholicism, treated so often by critics as an intrusion of Brontë's personal prejudice, stems from this sexual nexus. The intensity of her response is signalled initially by her seemingly excessive reactions to the nightly 'lecture pieuse': 'it made me so burning hot, and my temples and my heart and my wrist throbbed so fast, and my sleep afterwards was so broken with excitement, that I could sit no longer' (p. 163). The description of the content of the tales helps explain Lucy's extreme response: they contain 'the dread boasts of confessors, who had wickedly abused their office, trampling to deep degradation high-born ladies, making of countesses and princesses the most tormented slaves under the sun'. It is this 'abuse of office' which Lucy most fears: the subjection of the self to a male authority consequent on the revelation of the inner self. The explicit sexual nature of this subjection is suggested by the only named tale, that of Elizabeth of Hungary, whose source for Brontë was Charles Kingsley's virulently anti-Catholic poem *The Saint's Tragedy*.[19] The poem chronicles the effects, in Kingsley's view, of the 'Manichean contempt' for sexuality of the Roman Catholic church: Elizabeth's guilt concerning sexual desire leads to her total subjection to her priest, whose motives are seen to be an unsavoury mixture of sexual lust, worldly ambition and crude love of power.

In constructing Lucy's self-contradictory narrative, with its displacements, evasions and ghostly sightings, which clearly signal to the modern reader the presence of sexual repression, Brontë was not unconsciously articulating patterns in the human psyche which were to remain unrecognised, or even untheorised, until the advent of Freud. Sexuality, and specifically female sexuality, was frequently cited as a primary cause of nervous disorder and insanity in nineteenth-century discussions of mental illness. Ideas of women's sexual neurasthenia, as exemplified in Acton's writings, were directly counterpointed by theories of female psychology which stressed women's 'vulnerability': the mysterious processes of menstruation (whose causes remained, for the mid-Victorians, threatingly inexplicable), childbirth and lactation, which linked them to the natural world, also predisposed them, physiologically, to passion.[20] In the seventeenth century, William Harvey had drawn a comparison between women and animals in heat, observing that 'in like manner women occasionally become insane through ungratified desire'. They are saved only through 'good nurture', and innate modesty.[21] Virtually the same sentiments were repeated in the nineteenth century by the progressive alienist John Bucknill: 'Religious and moral principles alone give strength to the female mind', he observed. 'When these are weakened or removed by disease, the subterranean fires become active, and the crater gives forth smoke and flame'[22] (a process which is literally embodied by Brontë in the burning of Thornfield by the demonic Mrs Rochester, and in the outbreak of fire in the theatre as the 'fallen angel' Vashti is acting).

The idea of a specific sexual cause of mental disorder reappeared with renewed force in the nineteenth century following the work of Pinel (acknowledged founder of the new 'humanitarian' treatment of the insane), who suggested that mental alienation might proceed, not from an organic disease of the brain, but rather from a 'moral' (or functional) disorder.[23] His influential study of mental alienation stressed sexuality as a major factor in hysteria (a disorder which, although no longer attributed to the wanderings of the womb, was still recognised as a primarily female province). Medical texts of the nineteenth century emphasised repeatedly that hysteria occurred mainly in young, unmarried women.[24]

By the mid-century, commentators, eschewing earlier coyness, directly addressed the possible destructive consequences of continence. Thus Feuchtersleben argued, for example, in *The Principles of Medical Psychology* (1845, Eng. trans 1847), that hysteria arose most frequently in women from 'the want of exercise in those sexual functions intended by nature for use and disappointed desire or hope'.[25] The equation of women's 'natural' state and sexual activity figures even more decisively in Robert Carter's study *On the Pathology and Treatment of Hysteria* (1853), which outlines the first systematic theory of repression. Carter argues that the suppression of sexual passion is one of the primary causes of hysteria, and women, both by nature and social convention, are rendered more susceptible than men. Although woman is 'much under [the] dominion' of sexual desire, 'if unmarried and chaste, [she] is compelled to restrain every manifestation of its sway'.[26] While Harvey extolled the 'good nurture' and 'innate modesty' of women which enabled them to 'tranquilise the inordinate passions of the mind', Carter turns this formulation on its head, to show how social conventions of female passivity actually produce insanity.

Brontë's endorsement of Carter's position is clearly revealed in *Shirley*, where the disappointed Caroline, denied the social right to address her lover, reflects on the life of the old maid, comparing it directly to the life-denying existence of nuns, 'with their close cell, their iron lamp, their robe strait as a shroud, their bed narrow as a coffin ... these having violated nature, their natural likings and antipathies are reversed: they grow altogether morbid'.[27] Denial of sexuality is explicitly associated with the violation of nature. As in Carter's theory of repression, natural energies, if thwarted, turn back on themselves to create perverted forms. The attractive Caroline is not permitted to become 'morbid'. She is subjected instead to the physical ailment of brain fever which allows her mental faculties and personality to remain fundamentally intact.[28] In *Villette*, by contrast, Brontë actively explores the mental effects of repression, exposing, through the twists and turns of her narrative, the morbid processes of mind of her designedly uncongenial 'Miss Frost'.[29]

The question of Lucy's actual instability must remain unanswered if we, as readers, are to avoid falling into the error of Dr John in assuming unproblematic access to a realm of hidden 'truth'. It is possible, however, to trace the degree to which Lucy, in analysis of her own history, draws on the constructions of appropriate and 'insane' feminine behaviour to be found in mid-nineteenth-century psychological science. In her explicit use of contemporary scientific terms, Lucy draws attention to the explanatory complexes which underpin the often unconscious associations that direct her interpretation of behaviour. Her first noticeable use of scientific terminology occurs in her judgement on what she perceives to be the emotional excesses of the child Polly's behaviour with regard to her father: 'This, I perceived, was a one-idead nature; betraying that mono-maniac tendency I have ever thought the most unfortunate with

which man or woman can be cursed' (p. 16). The idea of monomania, displaced here onto Polly, is later appropriated by Lucy for
herself to describe her distress at losing Dr John's letter: '"Oh! they
have taken my letter!" cried the grovelling, groping, monomaniac'
(p. 353).[30] The 'curse' of monomania to which Lucy here refers was
first defined by Esquirol as an 'anormal condition of the physical or
moral sensibility, with a circumscribed and fixed delirium' (p. 200).
In the more developed definition of James Prichard, the chief
populariser of Esquirol's theories in England, monomania was seen
as a form of 'partial insanity, in which the understanding is partially
disordered or under the influence of some particular illusion, referring to one subject, and involving one train of ideas, while the
intellectual powers appear, when exercised on other subjects, to be in
a great measure unimpaired'.[31] Monomania was thus a form of
insanity, unmarked by mania, which could exist within the compass
of normal life. Esquirol's categories of insanity were founded on
assumptions of 'feminine vulnerability'. Women, he believed, were
more susceptible, both physiologically and psychologically, to religious and erotic melancholy, and hence to the 'hallucinations the
most strange and frequent' (p. 109) of religious and erotic monomania (a conjunction of religion and sexuality which clearly lies
behind the figure of the nun).

Lucy's monomania follows the course of Esquirol's erotic monomania, which he defines as a literal disease, a 'chronic cerebral
affection . . . characterised by an excessive passion' (p. 335). Reflecting the cultural attitudes of his era, Esquirol divides sexual afflictions
into chaste erotomania, whose origins lie in the imagination, and
'obscene', 'shameful and humiliating' nymphomania and satyriasis,
which originate in the organs of reproduction. Erotomaniacs' affections are 'chaste and honourable'; they 'never pass the limits of
propriety'. Instead, they tend to 'forget themselves; vow a pure, and
often secret devotion to the object of their love; make themselves
slaves to it; execute its orders with a fidelity often puerile; and obey
also the caprices that are connected with it' (p. 336). The description
offers an outline of Lucy's 'chaste', obsessional behaviour; her
devotion to Dr John, like that of the erotomaniac, is secret.

Esquirol's formulation of erotomania, like his other categories of
insanity, dresses recognised social stereotypes in the authority of
science. In his hands, the disease becomes socially respectable.
Erotomaniacs, he insists, do not, even in fantasy, seek fulfilment of
their desires: 'The erotomaniac neither desires, nor dreams even, of

the favours to which he might aspire from the object of his insane tenderness' (p. 336). The social repression, so evident in Lucy's narrative, which forbade women the articulation, or even conscious acknowledgement, of their desires, is encoded in his very definition of the disease. Esquirol's theory of erotomania, however, does not merely reinforce accepted social wisdom: chaste, hopeless passion is transformed into a cerebral disease, and must henceforth be treated as a possible symptom of insanity. The fear of mental illness signalled by Lucy's references to monomania underpins all her narrative: insanity is no longer limited to the recognisably disruptive forces of sexual desire, which may be locked away in the attic, but lurks as an incipient threat even in the 'chaste' repressed imaginings of the 'respectable' woman.

The structure of *Jane Eyre* had seemed to vindicate the mid-Victorian ideological position that successful regulation of the mental economy would lead to material social success. Bertha is sent to her death so that Jane can achieve the bourgeois dream. *Villette*, a more radical work than *Jane Eyre*, refuses this compromise. The novel calls into question the doctrine of control, thus implicitly challenging the economic model of healthy regulation which underpinned mid-Victorian theories of social, psychological, and physiological functioning. The mind, like the body, or the social economy, was to be treated as a system to be guided, regulated and controlled. As John Elliotson observed, 'the laws of the mind are precisely those of the functions of all other organs, – a certain degree of excitement strengthens it; too much exhausts it'.[32] In the mental as in the social economy, the aim must be to obtain maximum efficiency, neither overstretching nor underdeploying the natural resources. Theories of insanity drew on this model. Whether the cause were seen to be physical or moral, menstrual irregularities or the exclusive direction of the efforts of the mind into one channel, the net effect was that of unbalancing the body's natural economy which was founded on the free flow of 'secretions' and a hierarchical regulation of the mental forces.[33] Such theories of the bodily economy were based, however, on normative, gender-specific, codes of social behaviour. The social construction of insanity went hand in hand with that of femininity.

Lucy, in her vocabulary, seems initially to endorse enthusiastically the world view propounded by contemporary alienists and phrenologists, that cultivation of the correct faculties and suppression of the troublesome lower propensities would lead directly to social advancement. Launched in her teaching career she feels satisfied 'I was getting on; not lying the stagnant prey of mould and rust, but polishing my faculties and whetting them to a keen edge with constant use' (p. 113).[34] Such confidence soon dissolves, however, to be replaced by a rather different theory of social and psychological life. Brontë still uses the vocabulary of regulation and control, but to rather different effect. Lucy's efforts at regulation are no longer seen to be healthful. She strives for a literal form of live burial, recapitulating the experience of the nun: 'in catalepsy and a dead trance, I studiously held the quick of my nature' (p. 152). In a world where inner energies, when duly regulated, can find no external outlet, it is better, Lucy argues, that they be suppressed, if they are not to become self-consuming. Alternatively, they should be allowed to range in the world of fantasy. Thus she deliberately rejects Hag Reason, for the saving spirit of the imagination (p. 327), while the 'Real' – that realm to which the moral managers sought so assiduously to return their patients – is figured for her in the iconography of the fallen women: 'Presently the rude Real burst coarsely in – all evil, grovelling, and repellent as she too often is' (p. 153). The description, which prefigures the emergence of that 'grovelling, groping, monomaniac' Lucy herself, suggests the consequences for women of living according to male-defined reality (the 'Real' here is the casket containing the love letter which simultaneously dismisses Lucy as a sexual possibility and condemns her as a monster). Lucy's narrative, which dissolves the real into the imaginary, challenges male constructions of the social and psychological world.

This is not to suggest, however, that Lucy thereby steps entirely outside the formulations of psychological experience to be found in contemporary science. Her descriptions of her sufferings during the long vacation follow medical wisdom in assigning both physical and moral causes for this 'strange fever of the nerves and blood' (p. 222). Her sexual fantasies and nightmares of rejection are underpinned by the responsiveness of her physical frame to the storms and tempests outside, held by contemporary alienists to occasion and exacerbate insanity (see Graham, p. 392; Esquirol, p. 31). In thus projecting herself as a physical system, at the mercy of external physical changes, Lucy is able to deny her responsibility for her mental disorder: it is her 'nervous system' which cannot stand the strain; the controlling rational ego is dissolved into the body. The figure of the cretin, however, with its 'propensity ... to evil' (p. 220), stands as a warning projection of a model of mind where the physical is dominant, and the passions and propensities are not subject to any mental restraint.

Lucy seems to shift in and out of physiological explanation of the self at her convenience. In opposition to Dr John, she denies understanding his diagnosis: 'I am not quite sure what my nervous system is, but I was dreadfully low-spirited' (p. 261). Her attempt to define why she went to confession is marked by a similar resistance: 'I suppose you will think me mad for taking such a step, but I could not help it: I suppose it was all the fault of what you call my "nervous system"' (p. 264). Lucy's resistance to Dr John seems to stem less from the actual content of his medical verdicts than from his reduction of her to a bundle of symptoms, open to his professional definition and control.

Her battle for control over self-definition and interpretation of the processes of her own mind is not conducted solely with Dr John; the fiery M. Paul also enters the lists. On encountering Lucy in the art gallery after her illness, M. Paul berates her for her unfeminine behaviour in not being able to look after the cretin: 'Women who are worthy the name', he proclaims, 'ought infinitely to surpass our coarse, fallible, self-indulgent sex, in the power to perform such duties' (p. 290). The covert subject of this conversation is clearly the model of the female mind which suggested that women are more 'naturally' able than men to suppress their 'evil propensities'. Lucy, in self-defence, resorts to another male model of the female mind, asserting a physical illness: 'I had a nervous fever: my mind was ill' (p. 290). Diminished responsibility, which figured so largely in mid-Victorian trials of female criminals, becomes the basis of her excuse for 'unwomanly' conduct. Unlike Dr John, M. Paul refuses to accept this model of the mind and so draws attention back again to his own image of the constitution of the feminine. Dismissing the idea of nervous fever, he points instead to Lucy's 'temerity' in gazing at the picture of Cleopatra. The portrait of the fleshy Cleopatra, and the four pictures of 'La vie d'une femme', 'cold and vapid as ghosts', which M. Paul prefers for Lucy's instruction in the arts of femininity, take on iconographic significance in the narrative, representing the two alternative models for womanhood created by men.[35] Lucy's challenge to these models, implicit throughout her narrative, takes decisive form in the Vashti section.

The narrative sequence which culminates in the performance of Vashti actually starts, not in the theatre, but with Lucy's apparent sighting, that evening, of the nun. Dr John, refusing to respect her reticence, invokes once more his professional authority to diagnose the symptoms of her 'raised look', thus provoking Lucy's angry dismissal of his explanation: 'Of course with him, it was held to be another effect of the same cause: it was all optical illusion – nervous malady, and so on. Not one bit did I believe him; but I dared not contradict; doctors are so self-opinionated, so immovable in their dry, materialist views' (p. 368). Lucy rejects the 'doctor's' opinion on principle, although his physiological explanation appears perhaps surprisingly close to views she herself has expressed elsewhere. The grounds of her objection to Dr John's 'dry' materialism are made explicit, however, in her analysis of their mutual responses to the performance of Vashti.

For Lucy, Vashti on stage transcends socially imposed sex roles; she is neither woman nor man, but a devil, a literal embodiment of inner passion: 'Hate and Murder and Madness incarnate, she stood' (p. 369). Lucy's response is to invoke the male author of a rather different image of womanhood: 'Where was the artist of the Cleopatra? Let him come and sit down and study this different version. Let him seek here the mighty brawn, the muscle, the abounding blood, the full-fed flesh he worshipped: let all materialists draw nigh and look on' (p. 370). In a significant elision, Lucy has drawn together the materialism of doctors who seek to explain the processes of the mind with reference only to the physiological behaviour of the nerves, and the materialism of men who construct their images of women with reference only to the physical attributes of the flesh. The creation of the feminine in male-executed art is directly allied to the medical construction of women.

Lucy perceives, in Vashti, a force which could re-enact the miracle of the Red Sea, drowning Paul Peter Rubens (*sic*) and 'all the army of his fat women', but Dr John remains unresponsive to her challenge. He replicates, in the 'intense curiosity' with which he watches her performance, the professional gaze he has recently imposed on Lucy. His verdict underscores, for Lucy, his indifference to the inner movements of female experience: 'he judged her as a woman, not an artist: it was a branding judgement' (p. 373). Dr John's response is determined entirely by predefined categories of suitable female behaviour. As in his medical practice, he is insulated from any attempt to understand the causes or experiential detail of the cases he is examining through his possession of a socially validated system of classification which allows him to speak with unreflecting authority. Like his counterparts in the Book of Esther (from where the name Vashti is drawn), he trusts to the codification of male power to protect him from the 'demonic' challenge of female energy. (Queen

Vashti's refusal to show her beauty to the people at the king's command had provoked, from a worried male oligarchy, a proclamation 'into every province according to the writing thereof, and to every people after their language, that every man should bear rule in his own house' [Esther, 1:22]).

In choosing to equate medical and artistic constructions of the female identity through the notion of 'materialism', Brontë was drawing on the terms of contemporary debate. As an artistic term, implying the 'tendency to lay stress on the material aspects of the objects represented', the word materialism seems to date only from the 1850s (*O.E.D.*). Although the philosophical usage of materialism dates back to the eighteenth century, it had, at the time of Brontë's writing, become the focus of a virulent social and theological debate concerning the development of psychological theories which stressed that the brain was the organ of mind. Phrenology and mesmerism were located, in the popular press, at the centre of this controversy, as evidenced by the 1851 *Blackwood's* article which inveighed against the phreno-mesmerism of authors who believed that 'upon the materialism of life rest the great phenomena of what we were wont to call mind'.[36] Lucy's objections to materialism are not based on the religious grounds of contemporary debate; nor, as her own use of physiological vocabulary demonstrates, are they founded on an opposition to physiological explanation of the mind per se. Her rejection of medical and artistic materialism stems rather from the rigid and incomplete nature of their conception; she objects less to the idea of an interrelationship between body and mind than to their rather partial vision of this union. Under the medical and artistic gaze, woman is *reduced* to flesh and the material functioning of nerves.

In describing the impact of Vashti, Lucy herself employs the vocabulary of contemporary physiological psychology; Vashti's acting, 'instead of merely irritating imagination with the thought of what *might* be done, at the same time fevering the nerves because it was *not* done, disclosed power like a deep, swollen, winter river, thundering in cataract, and bearing the soul, like a leaf, on the steep and steely sweep of its descent' (p. 371). The term 'irritating' here is a technical one as used, for example, in Graham's observation that 'the nervous headache generally occurs in persons with a peculiar irritability of the nervous system' (p. 332). Coupled with the idea of 'fevering the nerves', it suggests two different levels of response within the nervous system, while the concluding imagery of the thundering river draws on physiological ideas of channelled energy within the brain. The power disclosed is both internal and external: it describes the force of Vashti's own inner energy, and the impact on the observer, Lucy. In this metaphorical usage of contemporary physiological theory, Brontë dramatises an even closer integration of body and mind than physiology envisaged, while simultaneously breaking down traditional boundaries of the self. Mind is not reduced to body, it becomes literally 'embodied', as Lucy earlier observed: 'To her, what hurts becomes immediately embodied: she looks on it as a thing that can be attacked, worried down, torn in shreds. Scarcely a substance herself, she grapples to conflict with abstractions. Before calamity she is a tigress; she rends her woes, shivers them in convulsed abhorrence' (p. 370). While the artist reduces woman to a material expanse of flesh, and the doctor to a mere encasement of nerves, Vashti reveals a true union between the worlds of mind and body: abstractions, the experiential details of mental life which physiology cannot describe, are given material form. In her treatment of Vashti, as throughout the novel, Brontë actually employs contemporary physiological theory to break through the narrow definition of the self it proposes.

The description of Vashti tearing hurt into shreds anticipates Lucy's later destruction of the figure of the nun:

> All the movement was mine, so was all the life, the reality, the substance, the force; as my instinct felt. I tore her up – the incubus! I held her on high – the goblin! I shook her loose – the mystery! And down she fell – down all round me – down in shreds and fragments – and I trode upon her.
>
> (p. 681)

Like Vashti, Lucy undertakes a material destruction of an inner hurt: the force and *substance* are Lucy's own.[37] The term 'incubus', with its associations of sexuality and mental disturbance, draws together the arenas of physical and mental life. In nineteenth-century psychological usage, incubus had become synonymous with nightmare. In a passage noted by Patrick Brontë in his *Domestic Medicine*, Robert Macnish observed, in *The Philosophy of Sleep*, that it was possible to suffer nightmare while awake and in 'perfect possession of [the] faculties'. Macnish records that he had 'undergone the greatest tortures, being haunted by spectres, hags, and every sort of phantom – having, at the same time, a full consciousness that I was labouring under incubus, and that all the terrifying objects around me were the creations of my own brain'.[38] Brontë takes this idea of waking nightmare, or incubus, one stage further, giving it a literal embodiment in her fiction which defies attempts to demarcate the boundaries between 'creations of the brain' and external forms.

Brontë offers, in *Villette*, a thorough materialisation of the self. The construct 'Lucy' is not a unified mental entity, located within a physiological frame, but rather a continuous process which extends beyond the confines of the flesh. Lucy's entire mode of self-articulation breaks down the hierarchy of outer and inner life upon which definitions of the 'Real' (and sanity) depend. Her description of the death of Hope for instance, parallels that of the literal burial of the letters: 'In the end I closed the eyes of my dead, covered its face, and composed its limbs with great calm' (p. 421). The burial itself is figured as the wrapping of grief in a 'winding-sheet'. Later, as Lucy pauses beside the grave, she recalls 'the passage of feeling therein buried' (p. 524). Metaphor has become inoperable; it functions, as Lucy's text makes clear, only if the speaker endorses normative social demarcations between different states. Thus the classrooms which initially only 'seem' to Lucy to be like jails quickly become 'filled with spectral and intolerable memories, laid miserable amongst their straw and their manacles' (p. 652). The controlling distance of 'seems' is collapsed, as 'memories', normally restricted to the realm of the mind, take on vivid physical form.

Lucy's intricate dramatisations of her feelings undermine traditional divisions between external social process and inner mental life, revealing their fictional status.[39] Her tale of Jael, Sisera and Heber, for example, simultaneously portrays physiological pain, psychological conflict, and the social drama of repression. Speaking of her desire to be drawn out of her present existence, Lucy observes:

> This longing, and all of a similar kind, it was necessary to knock on the head; which I did, figuratively, after the manner of Jael to Sisera, driving a nail through their temples. Unlike Sisera, they did not die: they were but transiently stunned, and at intervals would turn on the nail with a rebellious wrench; then did the temples bleed, and the brain thrill to its core.
>
> (p. 152)

The distinction between figural and literal quickly fades, as the inner psychic drama develops, the rebellious desires themselves perpetuate their torture, in a description which captures the physiological and psychological experience of socially inflicted repression (the term 'thrill' carried the medically precise meaning, in the mid-nineteenth century, of 'vibratory movement, resonance, or murmur').

The famous account of Lucy's opiate-induced wanderings into the night landscape of Villette also dissolves the divisions between inner and outer realms, as social experience now takes on the qualities of mental life, defying the normal boundaries of time and space. Amidst the physical forms of Cleopatra's Egypt, Lucy witnesses the figures of her inner thoughts parade before her eyes. Even here, however, where she seems most free from external social controls, she is still subject to fears of surveillance: she feels Dr John's gaze 'oppressing' her, seeming ready to grasp 'my identity . . . between his never tyrannous, but always powerful hands' (p. 661). As dominant male, and doctor, empowered by society to diagnose the inner movements of mind, and legislate on mental disease, Dr John threatens Lucy's carefully nurtured sense of self. Identity, as Brontë has shown throughout *Villette*, is not a given, but rather a tenuous process of negotiation between the subject and surrounding social forces.

The opposition to male materialism, voiced by Lucy in her confrontation with medical authority, gives dramatic expression to the interrogation of male constructions of the female psyche which underpins the narrative form of *Villette*. In seeking to avoid the surveillance of religious, educational and medical figures, trying to render herself illegible, Lucy attempts to assume control over the processes of her own self-definition. Yet her narrative, as I have argued, reveals a clear internalisation of the categories and terms of contemporary medical psychology. Lucy employs physiological explanations of mental life and appropriates to herself theories of a female predisposition to neurosis and monomania. In creating the autobiography of her troubled heroine, whose commitment to evasion and displacement is articulated in the very title of her book, Brontë explores both the social implications of contemporary psychological theory and its inner consequences. The form of her account, with its dissolution of divisions between inner psychological life and the material social world, suggests an alternative vision – one that challenges the normative psychological vision implicit in male definitions of the 'Real'.

From *One Culture: Essays in Science and Literature*, ed. George Levine (Madison, Wisconsin, 1987), pp. 313–35.

NOTES

[This essay first appeared in a collection of essays designed to explore the interaction between the discourses of science and literature. New Historicism is particularly suited to such an endeavour since it seeks to situate the text in its historical context and examine the ways in which the ideological divisions and tensions of a period are manifest in the inconsistencies of the text. So, for example, Sally Shuttleworth examines Lucy's use of the language of contemporary science in her analysis of self and argues that while Lucy internalises its negative strictures in some ways, she also subverts it through a narrative that 'challenges the normative psychological vision implicit in male definitions of the "Real"'. In recognising identity as a construct rather than a given, Shuttleworth's position is more closely aligned to the deconstructive reading of Mary Jacobus (see p. 121 above) than to earlier feminist readings which see Lucy's narrative as the courageous affirmation of an essential self. Ed.]

1. Charlotte Brontë, *Villette*, ed. H. Rosengarten and M. Smith (Oxford, 1984), p. 531.

2. Sandra Gilbert and Susan Gubar, *The Madwoman in the Attic: The Woman Writer and the Nineteenth-Century Literary Imagination* (New Haven, 1979), p. 360.

3. See Michel Foucault, *The Birth of the Clinic* (London, 1973), chs 7–9; and L. J. Jordanova, 'Natural Facts: A Historical Perspective on Science and Sexuality', in C. P. MacCormack and M. Strathern (eds), *Nature, Culture and Gender* (Cambridge, 1980).

4. Two works in the Keighley Mechanics' Institute, where the Brontës borrowed books, offer, for example, extensive discussions of the relationship between 'spectral illusion' and insanity: John Abercrombie, *Inquiries Concerning the Intellectual Powers* (Edinburgh, 1832), and Robert Macnish, *The Philosophy of Sleep* (Glasgow, 1830).

5. See R. Hunter and I. Macalpine, *Three Hundred Years of Psychiatry, 1535–1860* (Oxford, 1963), p. 1059.

6. For a discussion of George Eliot's indebtedness, see S. Shuttleworth, *George Eliot and Nineteenth-Century Science: The Make-Believe of a Beginning* (Cambridge, 1984). Wilkie Collins's relationship to contemporary psychology is the subject of a book by Jenny Taylor, forthcoming from Methuen.

7. Thomas John Graham, *Modern Domestic Medicine* (London, 1826). This work was in the Brontë Parsonage Museum, together with several other of the Reverend Brontë's medical books.

8. Quoted in V. Skultans, *Madness and Morals: Ideas on Insanity in the Nineteenth Century* (London, 1975), p. 172.

9. For an account of this transition and the development of 'moral management' in England see A. T. Scull, *Museums of Madness: The Social Organization of Insanity in Nineteenth-Century England* (London, 1979); M. Foucault, *Madness and Civilization: A History of Insanity in the Age of Reason*, trans. R. Howard (London, 1971); and R. Smith, *Trial by Medicine: Insanity and Responsibility in Victorian Trials* (Edinburgh, 1981).

10. Smith, ibid., p. 35.

11. 'What is Mesmerism?' *Blackwood's*, 70 (1851), 84.

12. A. T. Scull, *Museums of Madness* (London, 1979), p. 72.

13. See E. Showalter, 'Victorian Women and Insanity', *Victorian Studies*, 23 (1980), 166.

14. See L. J. Jordanova, 'Natural Facts' in C. P. MacCormack and M. Strathern (eds), *Nature, Culture and Gender* (Cambridge, 1980) and R. Smith, *Trial by Medicine* (Edinburgh, 1981), ch. 7.

15. J. E. D. Esquirol, *Mental Maladies: A Treatise on Insanity*, trans. E. K. Hunt (1845; rpt New York, 1965), p. 48.

16. See R. Smith, *Trial by Medicine*, ch. 7.

17. E. Showalter, 'Victorian Women and Insanity', p. 175.

18. M. Foucault, *Discipline and Punish: The Birth of the Prison*, trans. A. Sheridan (Harmondsworth, 1979), pp. 202–3.

19. J. Carlisle, 'A Prelude to *Villette*: Charlotte Brontë's Reading, 1850–52', *Bulletin of Research in the Humanities*, 82 (1979), 409. For Brontë's response to the poem, see T. J. Wise and J. A. Symington, *The Brontës: Their Lives, Friendships and Correspondence*, 4 vols (Oxford, 1932), vol. 3, pp. 268–9.

20. John Elliotson, whose work the Reverend Brontë commends in his copy of Graham, observes in *Human Physiology*, 5th edn (London, 1840) that the source of menstrua is entirely unclear.

21. Quoted in R. Hunter and I. Macalpine, *Three Hundred Years of Psychiatry*, p. 131.

22. Quoted in E. Showalter, 'Victorian Women and Insanity', p. 167.

23. See I. Veith, *Hysteria: The History of a Disease* (Chicago, 1965), pp. 175–84.

24. See R. Macnish, *Philosophy of Sleep*, pp. 139, 143, and George Man Burrows, *Commentaries on Insanity* (1828), quoted in V. Skultans, *Madness and Morals* (London, 1975), p. 226.

25. Quoted in I. Veith, *Hysteria: The History of a Disease*, p. 191.

26. Quoted in ibid., p. 201.

27. Charlotte Brontë, *Shirley*, ed. H. Rosengarten and M. Smith (Oxford, 1979), vol. 2, pp. 440–1.

28. Although Caroline's illness is never specifically defined as 'brain fever', it carries all the usual symptoms. See A. C. Peterson, 'Brain Fever in Nineteenth-Century Literature: Fact and Fiction', *Victorian Studies*, 19 (1976), 439–64.

29. Brontë's original name for Lucy was 'Frost'. As she observes in a letter to W. S. Williams (6 November 1852): 'A cold name she must have ... for she has about her an external coldness'. See *The Brontës: Their Lives, Friendships and Correspondence*, vol. 4, p. 18.

30. The edition here actually reads 'monamaniac'. I presume, however, that this is a printing error.

31. J. C. Prichard, *A Treatise on Insanity and Other Disorders Affecting the Mind* (1837; rpt New York, 1973), p. 16.

32. J. Elliotson, *Human Physiology*, p. 37.

33. These were two of the causes cited by T. J. Graham, *Modern Domestic Medicine*, p. 392.

34. Her vocabulary is precisely that employed in the annual report of the Keighley Mechanics' Institute in 1832: 'The faculties of the mind can only be preserved in a sound and healthful state by constant exercise ... as the metallic instrument corrodes and wastes with indolence and sloth, so with continued use, an edge is produced capable of cutting down every obstacle.'

35. For an analysis of the functions of these paintings see S. Gilbert and S. Gubar, *The Madwoman in the Attic*, p. 420.

36. 'What is Mesmerism?' *Blackwood's*, 70 (1851), 81.

37. Mary Jacobus, in her excellent article on *Villette*, offers a slightly different reading of this passage: see 'The Buried Letter: Feminism and Romanticism in *Villette*', in *Women Writing and Writing about Women* (London, 1979), p. 54. [Reprinted in this volume – see p. 121. Ed.]

38. R. Macnish, *The Philosophy of Sleep*, p. 136.

39. As Inga-Stina Ewbank has observed in *Their Proper Sphere: A Study of the Brontë Sisters as Early Victorian Novelists* (London, 1966), the personifications, lengthened into allegories of Lucy's emotional crises, 'do not arrest the action of *Villette*, for in a sense they *are* the action; even more than in *Jane Eyre* the imagery of *Villette* tends to act out an inner drama which superimposes itself on, or even substitutes for external action' (p. 189).

Further Reading

Charlotte Brontë was capable of shrewd criticism of her own work. Her letters provide ample evidence of her sound judgements on a variety of literary matters – the need to give up the fantasy world of her juvenilia, the sexist nature of contemporary criticism, her strengths and weaknesses as a writer, and the relative merits of her publishers' advice. Students might start their survey of Brontë criticism, then, with the following works:

Christine Alexander, *The Early Writings of Charlotte Brontë* (Oxford: Basil Blackwell, 1983).

Elizabeth Gaskell, *The Life of Charlotte Brontë* (1857; rpt Oxford: Oxford University Press, 1974).

T. J. Wise and J. A. Symington (eds), *The Brontës: Their Lives, Friendships and Correspondence*, 4 vols (Oxford: Shakespeare Head, 1932).

A perspective on the history of Brontë criticism is of particular interest to students concerned with the implications of gender in literary studies. Three collections of essays provide a helpful overview, and Ruth Gounelas's essay offers a useful commentary on critical fashions and prejudices:

Miriam Allott (ed.), *The Brontës: The Critical Heritage* (London: Routledge & Kegan Paul, 1974).

Miriam Allott (ed.), *Charlotte Brontë: 'Jane Eyre' and 'Villette'*, Casebook Series (London: Macmillan, 1973).

Ruth Gounelas, 'Charlotte Brontë and the Critics: Attitudes to the Female Qualities in her Writing', *Journal of the Australasian Universities Language and Literature Association*, 62 (1984), 151–70.

Ian Gregor (ed.), *The Brontës: A Collection of Critical Essays*, Twentieth Century Views (Englewood Cliffs, NJ: Prentice-Hall, 1970).

A number of critical studies help to place Brontë's work in its historical context. Most of the works listed below are written from a perspective informed by feminism:

Françoise Basch, *Relative Creatures: Victorian Women in Society and the Novel 1837–67*, trans. Anthony Rudolf (London: Allen Lane, 1974).

Harriet Bjork, *The Language of Truth: Charlotte Brontë, the Woman Question, and the Novel* (Lund, Sweden: Gleerup, 1974).

Vineta Colby, *The Singular Anomaly: Women Novelists of the Nineteenth Century* (London: University of London Press, 1970).

Inga-Stina Ewbank, *Their Proper Sphere: a Study of the Brontë Sisters as Early Victorian Novelists* (London: Edward Arnold, 1966).

Winifred Gérin, *Charlotte Brontë: the Evolution of Genius* (Oxford: Clarendon Press, 1967).

Pauline Nestor, *Female Friendships and Communities: Charlotte Brontë, George Eliot and Elizabeth Gaskell* (Oxford: Clarendon Press, 1985).

Tom Winnifrith, *The Brontës and their Background* (London: Macmillan, 1977).

This contextual study can be further expanded through the examination of the relation of Charlotte Brontë's work to various literary conventions:

Rachel M. Brownstein, *Becoming a Heroine: Reading About Women in Novels* (1982; rpt Harmondsworth: Penguin, 1984).

Janice Carlisle, 'The Face in the Mirror: Villette and the Conventions of Autobiography', *ELH*, 46 (1979), 262–89.

Rosemary Clark-Beattie, 'Fables of Rebellion: anti-Catholicism and the Structure of *Villette*', *ELH*, 53 (1986), 821–47.

Robert B. Heilman, 'Charlotte Brontë's "New" Gothic', in *The Victorian Novel: Modern Essays in Criticism*, ed. Ian Watt (New York: Oxford University Press, 1971), pp. 165–80.

Linda Hunt, 'Charlotte Brontë and the Suffering Sisterhood', *Colby Library Quarterly*, 19: 1 (1983), 7–17.

Annette Tromly, *The Cover of the Mask: The Autobiographers in Charlotte Brontë's Fiction* (Victoria, BC: University of Victoria, 1982).

The resurgence of interest in Charlotte Brontë's work in the last 20 years has seen considerable attention given to questions of style. Through close and sustained textual analysis a number of critics have challenged the frequently reductive view of Brontë as a 'fictionalised autobiographer', and stressed the artistry of Brontë's prose:

Jean Frantz Blackall, 'Point of View in *Villette*', *The Journal of Narrative Technique*, 6:1 (1976), 14–29.

Earl Knies, *The Art of Charlotte Brontë* (Athens, Ohio: Ohio University Press, 1969).

Karl Kroeber, *Styles in Fictional Structure: The Art of Jane Austen, Charlotte Brontë and George Eliot* (Princeton: Princeton University Press, 1971).

Margot Peters, *Style in the Novel* (Madison: University of Wisconsin Press, 1973).

Charlotte Brontë's life and novels have always provided a fertile ground for psychological examination. However, the amateur speculation of contemporary nineteenth-century critics has given way in recent times to more comprehensive psychoanalytic analyses:

Charles Burkhart, *Charlotte Brontë: a Psychosexual Study of her Novels* (London: Gollancz, 1973).
Robert Keefe, *Charlotte Brontë's World of Death* (Austin: University of Texas Press, 1979).
John Maynard, *Charlotte Brontë and Sexuality* (Cambridge: Cambridge University Press, 1984).
Margot Peters, *Unquiet Soul: a Biography of Charlotte Brontë* (London: Hodder & Stoughton, 1975).

The rise of feminist criticism has been the single most important factor in the revaluation of Charlotte Brontë's work that has taken place in the last 20 years. Earlier feminist accounts have tended to celebrate Brontë's achievement as a novelist and to see her heroines as exemplars of female courage and self-assertion:

Nina Auerbach, *Communities of Women: An Idea in Fiction* (Cambridge, Mass.: Harvard University Press, 1978).
Ellen Moers, *Literary Women* (New York: Doubleday, 1976).
Pauline Nestor, *Charlotte Brontë* (London: Macmillan, 1987).

More recently, Penny Boumelha has extended such feminist analysis by adding a critique of class and race to that of gender:

Penny Boumelha, *Charlotte Brontë* (Hemel Hempstead: Harvester Wheatsheaf, 1990).

Finally, three challenging works draw heavily on poststructuralist, deconstructive and psychoanalytic theorists to provide examples of the most theoretically sophisticated feminist analysis of Brontë's work:

Christina Crosby, 'Charlotte Brontë's Haunted Text', *Studies in English Literature*, 24 (1984), 701–15.
Margaret Homans, *Bearing the Word: Language and Female Experience in Nineteenth-Century Women's Writing* (Chicago: University of Chicago Press, 1986).
Patricia Yaeger, *Honey-mad Women: Emancipatory Strategies in Women's Writing* (New York: Columbia University Press, 1988).

Notes on Contributors

Terry Eagleton is Professor of English, Wadham College, Oxford University. His publications include *Myths of Power: A Marxist Study of the Brontës* (London, 1975); *Marxism and Literary Criticism* (London, 1976); *The Rape of Clarissa* (Oxford, 1982); *Literary Theory: An Introduction* (Oxford, 1982) and *The Ideology of the Aesthetic* (Oxford, 1990).

Sandra M. Gilbert is Professor of English Literature, University of California, Davis, and **Susan Gubar** is Professor of English Literature, Indiana University, Bloomington. Their publications include *The Madwoman in the Attic: The Woman Writer and the Nineteenth-Century Literary Imagination* (New Haven, 1979); *Shakespeare's Sisters: Feminist Essays on Women Poets* (Bloomington, 1979); and *The War of the Words* (New Haven, 1988) and *Sexchanges* (New Haven, 1989), which constitute the first two volumes of *No Man's Land: The Place of the Woman Writer in the Twentieth Century*, a three-book sequel to *The Madwoman in the Attic*. They have also edited *The Norton Anthology of Literature by Women* (New York, 1985).

Mary Jacobus is Anderson Professor of English Literature, Cornell University, Ithaca, New York. Her publications include *Tradition and Experiment in Wordsworth's Lyrical Ballads* (Oxford, 1976); *Reading Woman: Essays in Feminist Criticism* (New York, 1986); and *Romanticism, Writing and Sexual Difference: Essays on the Prelude* (Oxford, 1989). She has edited *Women Writing and Writing about Women* (London, 1979) and co-edited, with Evelyn Fox Keller and Sally Shuttleworth, *Body Politics: Women and the Discourses of Science* (London, 1990).

Kate Millett is an author. Her publications include *Sexual Politics* (New York, 1970); *The Prostitution Papers* (St Albans, 1975); *Flying* (New York, 1974); *Sita* (New York, 1977); and *Going to Iran* (New York, 1982).

Helen Moglen is Professor of English Literature, University of California, Kresge College, Santa Cruz. Her publications include *Charlotte Brontë: The Self Conceived* (New York, 1976).

Nancy Rabinowitz is Professor of Comparative Literature, Hamilton College, Clinton, New York. Her publications include numerous articles and a forthcoming book, *Euripides and the Traffic in Women*.

Sally Shuttleworth is a Lecturer in the School of English, University of Leeds. Her publications include *George Eliot and Nineteenth-Century Science* (Cambridge, 1984); and a critical edition of *The Mill on the Floss* (London, 1990). She is joint editor, with John Christie, of *Nature Transfixed: Science and Literature, 1700–1900* (Manchester, 1989); and with Mary Jacobus and Evelyn Fox Keller, of *Body Politics: Women and the Discourses of Science* (London, 1990).

Brenda Silver is Professor of English, Dartmouth College, Hanover, New Hampshire. Her publications include *Virginia Woolf's Reading Notebooks* (Princeton, 1983); and articles on Woolf, Forster, and Le Carré. She has co-edited, with Lynn Higgins, *Rape and Representation* (New York, 1991).

Tony Tanner is a Fellow of King's College, Cambridge. His publications include *The Reign of Wonder* (Cambridge, 1965); *City of Words* (London, 1971); *Adultery in the Novel: Contract and Transgression* (Baltimore, 1979); and *Scenes of Nature, Signs of Men* (Cambridge, 1987).

Index